The AUSTRALIAN Women's Weekly G

Roses
for every garden

By Trevor Nottle

Easily the most popular flower among gardeners, roses are loved and admired for their heady fragrance, graceful flowers, and rich variety of colours. Melded into a landscape, they can look simply glorious. But how to use them to create such a scene is the challenge. In this book you'll find practical and inspirational advice on planning a rose garden, selecting the right plants for your garden and using them to maximum effect, and caring for roses. Included, too, are simple design ideas which can easily be adapted for your garden so that everything will be coming up roses!

❖ ❖ ❖

Leigh Clapp

THE QUEEN OF FLOWERS

Adding a touch of distinction

Roses and gardens go together like sunshine and flowers. They brighten suburban gardens, flourish in sunny, inner-city terrace gardens and add fresh glories to historic homes. Planted singly or en masse, they are the flower that just about everyone recognises.

Today roses exist in a variety of habits of growth for use in a wide range of gardening situations. The bush and climbing roses of our parents' and grandparents' gardens have been reworked by rose breeders with wild roses and centuries-old garden roses from Europe and China. The result is a multitude of new roses, including groundcover roses, patio roses, modern shrub roses and "English Roses".

The flowers, as beautiful as ever, come in a array of colours with perfumes to match – fruity, spicy, aromatic or the familiar roses scent – and with a diversity of flower forms, from a single row of petals to densely packed doubles. In years gone by, the roses most sought after were those that produced one perfect flower on each stem for cut flowers and flower shows, now the aim of breeders is to produce roses that will flower prolifically over a long season by opening a succession of buds clustered in large heads. Resistance to pests and diseases has also been a focus for breeders, so now there are plenty of roses with these attributes.

In pots, borders or beds mixed with shrubs, perennials, bulbs and annuals; in cottage gardens and in formal gardens, roses add a touch of distinction that can only be bestowed by the queen of flowers. This book is designed to introduce such wonderful roses to you and show how they can be used to create beautiful, easy-care landscapes.

All plant dimensions are given in metric and imperial measurements. The conversions have been rounded off to the nearest whole number.

*'Madame Hardy' is an exquisite
old-fashioned rose with perfect
white petals folding inwards
towards a green pointel.*

*The thornless 'Zephirine Drouhin'
will soon clamber over this arch,
adorning it with fragrant blooms,
and inviting closer inspection.*

*Solid blocks of glorious colour,
achieved with 'Great News' (front)
and 'Gold Bunny', accentuate
a formal rose garden.*

*The glorious yellow 'Canary Bird'
has only one season of flower and few
hips, if any, but it's always a
delight in late spring.*

WILD ROSES
Through History

A fascination from the very beginning

Celebrated in poetry and art throughout the ages, the rose has become a universal symbol of beauty and love. Aphrodite, the Greek godess of love, is said to have adopted the rose as her personal emblem, and there are tales told of Cleopatra soaking the sails of her ship with rose water when she left Antony so that the winds would be as lovesick as she.

We do know that roses were used in religious ceremonies, funerals, banquets and pageants by the ancient Egyptians, by the Chinese and by the Greeks and Romans. Two hundred years before Christ, the rose was being cultivated extensively in northern Africa and southern Italy for export as flowers to Rome. The buds and petals were strewn at feasts and celebrations and woven into garlands and swags to decorate temples and

> ❧
> *"Surviving manuscripts, artworks, folk stories and songs ... display the people's admiration of roses."*
> ❧

palaces for important occasions.

But is impossible to say when roses from the wild were first brought into gardens.

Besides being grown as a horticultural crop, roses were used medicinally to make soothing eye washes and headache remedies; they were also important ingredients in the luxury perfume industries.

Wealthy Romans who had country villas enjoyed cultivating wild roses as part of their pleasure grounds. Pliny the Younger, a Roman aristocrat and author, described in his works how, with other flowering shrubs, roses could be used to make pleasing groves and walks.

Proletariat Romans, and the barbarian Goths, Britons and Gauls, gathered rose hips as a wild berry fruit and used them, and the petals, in homoeopathic remedies.

Roses also have long associations with the cultures of ancient China, India and Persia. Surviving manuscripts, artworks, folk stories and songs from these countries display the people's admiration of roses.

When early seafarers and traders returned to Europe with Middle Eastern and Asian ceramics and textiles decorated with motifs of strange and unusual roses, Europeans were captivated. Their imaginations spurred on by a few scraps of luxurious cloth, or designs on plates, Western gardeners began to dream about the marvels of roses from Asia; and they wanted them!

Roses collected in the wild, and rose plants collected from Turkish gardens, began to arrive in Europe through Vienna around 1600. The yellow rose, *Rosa foetida*, was one of the first. But it was not until the mid-18th century that Chinese garden roses began to arrive.

It was an exciting time for gardeners. Plant collectors were sent to China and the new colonies in North America to gather new species of roses. The new roses increased the range of colours and some forms were found that produced double flowers. Where wild roses, with their single row of petals, were once regarded as commonplace, they now became the objects of horticultural collectors. Double roses were regarded as rarities, to be sought regardless of cost; roses became fashionable.

Among the earliest to write about roses as decorative rarities as well as useful medicinal herbs was John Gerrard. *In The Herball or Generall Historie of Plantes* of 1633, he lavishes praise and most elaborate illustration on 'The great Holland Rose" (*Rosa centifolia* – the "hundred leav'd [petalled] rose").

In this rose, the decorative qualities of a double flower are more important than any medicinal use it may have. Gerrard also includes other double roses which have obvious garden appeal, and which can still be grown today as fine flowering shrubs – *Rosa alba* 'Semi-plena', *R. gallica* 'Tuscany', *R. foetida* 'Persiana', *R. cinnamonea* 'Plena' and *R. damascena*. These roses mark the transition from wild roses grown as garden plants to the carefully selected, double forms which exist only because of their appeal to keen-eyed gardeners through the centuries.

A THORNY QUESTION

Which roses are right for you?

With the words, "of course, we must have some roses", many of us have begun, with joyful anticipation, our first gardens. As new home owners, we're about to take that first step, drawn by the age-old, irresistible allure of the rose.

And so we set off to buy a few nice roses. If only it were that simple!

Too Many Beauties

There are dozens, often hundreds of roses to choose from, each with an eye-catching label and a seductive description. It's easy to be beguiled by descriptions of the "Premier Collection", "Landscaper's Best Six" and "Selected Cottage Garden Beauties". How do you choose from the array of stunning dark reds, luscious pinks, clear yellows, dreamy lilacs, snowy whites and alluring blends of scarlet and gold?

Ensnared by the lovely photographs and with dreams of creating our own glorious gardens, some of us take the plants home without a clue as to how those hues will meld into a satisfying landscape. And of course, they won't; a rainbow of mixed colours rarely works.

So how do we start our bed of roses while avoiding beginners' mistakes?

Think Now, Buy Later

The best way is to keep your hands in your pockets in those proud, early months of home making. Visit nurseries by all means, but then do some research and planning before you part with your cash. Consider your climate (read our advice on the best climate for roses on page 14); is yours a marginal or problem climate?

This will also guide your choice. Make some notes about the colours you like and which tones will enhance the appearance of your house. Visit neighbourhood and display gardens; observe how roses and other plants are combined to create a colour scheme, and how they are used to screen parts of the garden from the street, or from other parts of the garden. See how plants are used as groundcover, to spread down slopes and to drape over walls. Make a note about sun/shade conditions and soil types; think about what your garden will be used for; children's play, outdoor living and meals, quiet relaxation, or as a hobby in itself. Above all, think about how much work you want to put into making and maintaining your garden.

Now it is time to wonder where to put those roses and to select varieties that will meet the needs of your garden.

A gateway awash with blooms, including the dark pink of the wild rose Rosa chinensis 'Mutabilis' and the pale gold of 'Perle d'Or', provides a warm welcome.

'Altissimo' 3

'Bloomfield Abundance' 1

'Golden Wings' 2

'Tip Top'

'Nozomi'

Gary Aitchison (1) / Paddy Wales (2) / Leigh Clapp (3) / Garden Picture Library (4) / Rodney Hyett (5)

Landscaping with
ROSES

If you think of roses as having five basic profiles of growth, you will have a handy guide to filling in the spaces in your garden plans. Of course, it would be silly to try to use roses to answer every planning problem, but they should be considered alongside other plants when you are making your choices. Briefly, the five profiles are:

1 Roses with large shrub-like forms that stand alone as "look at me" specimens. They can also be used in colour groupings with other shrubs, either as background or as the main feature. Either way, use progressively lower plants around them to create a sloping "hill" of flower and foliage. 'Bloomfield Abundance' is the feature here and, below it in the foreground, is *Rosa chinesis* 'Mutabilis'.

2 Roses of medium shrubby growth, that act as major anchor points in a garden design. The solid cover of foliage and bulky "mass" of the roses give a sense of stability and permanence. 'Golden Wings' is a fine example of a fairly compact shrub rose that will grow to make a dome of foliage down to ground level.

3 Climbing roses come in all sizes, from giants that are capable of romping through forest trees to modest scramblers, such as this one, 'Altissimo', that is perfectly in scale with small suburban gardens. By selecting appropriate varieties, you can use climbing roses to transform unsightly garden sheds; they can also be neatly trained to lie flat against a decorative trellis.

4 Shrub roses of low growth, with their prolific, extended-flowering season, healthy compact growth and easy-care needs, can be successful choices for almost any sunny garden setting. The more compact low-growing forms are ideal for pots and, when teamed with potted annuals, perennials and bulbs, can make dull corners glow with colour. 'Tip Top' is a good example of a low, compact shrub rose.

5 Trailing and very low-growing (prostrate) roses are ideal for use as groundcover plants in exposed, sunny positions. Modern varieties offer an enormous range of colours and sizes. With extended flowering seasons and dense evergreen growth that resists pests and diseases, they can be also used to cascade over rockeries and retaining walls, as with 'Nozomi', shown here. Alternatively, some of the many forms of low-growing roses can be grown in hanging baskets, window boxes or pots.

A real charmer dating from 1909 is 'Grüss an Aachen'. A large-flowered bush rose with upright growth, it is suited to standardisation.

Don Brice

THREE EASY CATEGORIES

The best roses for landscaping purposes can be classified under three headings: wild roses and their near relatives; large-flowered bush roses; and modern shrub roses.

This simplified classification is much more convenient for the average gardener than trying to come to grips with the endlessly confusing "classes" of roses, such as "Hybrid Tea", "Grand-iflora", "Polyantha", "Bourbon", "Noisette", "Floribunda", "Gallica", "Alba" and so on, the names by which afficionados describe their treasures. These names have a romance of their own, but they don't set out which roses are really useful for what purposes.

Wild Roses and Their Near Relatives

Wild roses are called species roses by botanists and are those roses which occur naturally in the wild. Together with their near relatives, the wild or species hybrids, they contribute carefree, natural effects to gardens with their freedom of growth, prolific flowers and foliage that varies from light to heavy. In many cases, wild roses have at least two seasons of beauty; when they are in flower and when they are heavy with fruit (hips). And those

TWO BASIC SHAPES

Bush rose shape

Shrub rose shape

who enjoy beauty of form will also discern loveliness in the tracery of bare branches in winter and in the shapes when they are in leaf.

Large-Flowered Bush Roses and Climbing Roses

These are hybrid roses, that is, roses bred by deliberately crossing one variety with another. These roses have been bred to produce perfect flowers of a particular style, sometimes without much regard to how the plant performs in the garden. Hybridising repeatedly within the large-flowered group of roses produced a succession of varieties, from the large-flowered 19th century roses, such as Bourbons, Noisettes and Hybrid Perpetuals, to the 20th century Hybrid Teas and Floribun-das. More recent large-flowered roses have complex genetic backgrounds that usually involve Hybrid Teas and/or Floribundas being interbred with old European roses and even species roses.

Large-flowered bush roses have habits of growth and flowers that are well suited to formal-style gardens. Grown either as standards, that is, grown on a tall, single trunk, or as bushes, they have dignity and presence. Large-flowered climbing roses are most easily grown on trellises

The large, creamy yellow trusses of 'Penelope', a modern shrub rose, are enchanting, managing to outshine other flowering plants. Its positioning near a walkway means its strong fragrance, as well as flowers, will be enjoyed by passers-by.

from which they can be taken down for their annual pruning. You can combine them elegantly with formal plantings of bush roses, or use them to suggest the charm of a cottage in a more casual garden style.

Modern Shrub Roses

Modern shrub roses, which have been bred since the turn of the 19th century, are as genetically complex as the large-flowered bush roses, but they are distinguished by their stronger and more lax growth. Within two or three years of planting they grow into shrub proportions, whereas large-flowered bush roses are more compact and stiffly upright in their growth. The "English Roses" bred by David Austin are good representatives of modern shrub roses that have achieved popularity with rose

lovers around the world. But they are not the only model for the group. There are also very floriferous, more compact plants, such as the patio roses, and the low, vigorous and spreading groundcover roses, such as 'Flower Carpet'.

Overall, you can think of modern shrub roses as being shrubby in shape (as against "bush" roses) but variable in size. They have much of the freedom of habit and disease resistance of the wild roses, and plenty of flower power.

Modern shrub roses offer endless possibilities for use in formal and informal designs, and as they are further developed in the years ahead there will be more opportunities for imaginative gardening. Alert to the shrinking size of today's gardens, breeders of modern shrub roses are working hard to develop a varied range that will perform different functions in these miniature landscapes.

Leigh Clapp

The Allure of the Rose

Aside from all these perfectly good reasons for growing roses in our gardens, why is it that they spring so readily to mind when garden making comes to the fore in our lives?

"And of course we must have some roses" – yes, but why?

Apart from the stunning beauty of their flowers, they are tough, hardy, tolerant, adaptable and resistant to pests and diseases. But what is it about them that brings them first to mind when our thoughts turn to gardening? I think the special thing about them is that, throughout our collective history, European and Asian, they have always been

A pretty effect is achieved with a combination of the mauve 'Veilchenblau', the pale pink 'Francis E. Lester' and the scarlet 'Paul's Scarlet'; a mix of climbers and open shrubs assembled with flair.

with us in our gardens, in our religions, in our myths and legends, in our children's tales and folk stories, in our arts and in our daily lives. Their beauty and perfume have always gone hand in hand with civilisation as symbols of life, and death, and of life eternal.

BEST CLIMATE FOR ROSES

Growing roses in a range of conditions

There are almost as many opinions about the best climate for roses as there are rose growers! Enthusiasts from all rose-growing countries have conflicting views on what climate is best for roses.

Countries where the growing and flowering season is long, and the weather warm or hot and sunny, produce some of the best roses, usually in autumn when the heat of summer has passed. In other countries where the climate is mild or cool and the buds can develop slowly, spring roses have their passionate advocates as being the best.

So beginners may see that roses grow best in either warm or hot climates with dry summers, such as exist in parts of California, South and Western Australia, South Africa and the south of France, or in cool and mild climates, such as in England, New Zealand and in the cooler parts of the USA and western Canada.

But What is "Best"?

The best climate for roses is one where the plants grow and flower vigorously with few climate-induced diseases, such as mildew and black spot. Both of these are made worse by high humidity in spring and summer, coupled with poor air circulation. Gardeners in areas of low humidity have considerably less need to spray for these troublesome diseases; on the other hand their warm, dry air can encourage thrips and mites. Roses grown in areas that receive little or no summer rain will need a deep, soaking watering about once a month to perform well but can survive with less.

Nature Guides Us

Generally speaking, roses are very adaptable plants and will grow well enough in a huge range of cool, mild, warm and hot climates. In nature they are found mostly in the temperate parts of all three northern continents – not usually in the very cold places, neither in the deserts nor in the tropics.

Tropical and subtropical gardens, with their steamy days and warm nights, are not ideal rose-growing climates, and neither are areas where winter minimums plunge below -20°C (-4°F), though there are a few varieties that will thrive in these areas. For the best of these, See "Frost and Freeze Hardy Roses" on page 18, and for climbers, "Left Out in the Cold" on page 93.

Almost all of the roses described or listed in this book will grow well in a wide range of climates, other than the tropical and the very cold.

Most roses will take some very hot weather and also come through moderate frosts unscathed; those that are frost-tender are described as such and those that are frost-hardy are also indicated. Proofing roses against extreme cold is possible with heavy insulation of straw and mulch held tight against winter winds with wire and burlap. This technique is used in areas, such as central Canada where spring arrives in fits and starts with recurrent frosts in between.

There are plenty of rose collectors and exhibitors who grow roses in the colder parts of Canada and the USA; they are not fussed by all the work necessary to protect the plants from freezing, heaving and other winter damage. But it may be

*Heat-tolerant
and long-flowering,
'Duchesse de Brabant'
dates from 1857,
and is still found in
many gardens.*

more work than you are prepared to carry out just to have some roses in your garden! Likewise, gardeners in the tropics and subtropics have difficulties growing roses; the plants need very frequent spraying to ward off pests and diseases, and because they never get a proper resting period in winter, they grow continuously and can exhaust themselves to the point of death within three or four years of first being planted.

Weather vs Climate

Before closing this topic, we should ask: is climate the same thing as weather? While meteorologists may argue the finer points, it is useful to think of weather as the day-to-day events, and of climate as the pattern of those events over a long period, such as a year, or longer. Roses tolerate a wide range of weather patterns, but perform best when dry, sunny days outnumber cloudy, wet days, and when winds are gentle, stirring breezes rather than gusting blasts – high winds are always damaging to the growth and flowers of roses.

Strong winter winds, especially those that are very chilly, can dry out and scorch the canes of dormant roses. Roses need good spring rains to grow and flower well, but can get by with remarkably dry conditions once new growth has ripened – provided they are well mulched. In many instances additional watering will be necessary during hot, dry summers, but remember that roses do not need oceans of water to do well; if water must be supplied, use deep soaking weeks apart rather than frequent, shallow watering.

Heat-tolerant, 'Safrano' (left) and 'Comtesse du Cayla' (below).

In Extreme Climates, Seek the Strongest

These comments mainly relate to large-flowered bush roses, such as Hybrid Teas, Floribundas and Grandifloras, as these are the most highly promoted roses and therefore the most popular, believed by many beginner gardeners as the only roses worthy of growing.

If you want roses as part of your garden design, rather than as a collection of cosseted specimens, choose the types that are more suited to your climate; those from a different regime may be weakened by the change, making them more susceptible to pests and diseases.

The lists, "Frost and Freeze-Hardy Roses", on page 18, and "Heat-tolerant Roses" on page 19, contain roses known to be successful in either very cold or subtropical areas.

A good choice for the subtropics and full of charm, 'Parsons Pink China', has large clusters of flowers which are pale pink at first, then darkening to a rich pink.

CLIMATE ZONES

Our terms defined:

■ **COLD:** *where the temperature range can be from -10°C (14°F) in winter, to 20°C (69°F) in summer.*

■ **COOL:** *where the temperature range can be from 0°C (32°) in winter to 25°C (77°F) in summer.*

■ **MILD:** *where the temperature range can be from 10°C (51°F) in winter to 25°C (77°F) in summer.*

■ **WARM:** *where the temperature range can be from 10°C (51°F) in winter to 30° (87°F) in summer.*

■ **HOT:** *where the temperature range can be from 15°C (59°F) in winter to 30°C (87°F) and higher in summer.*

FROST AND FREEZE-HARDY ROSES

Choices for cold climates

Rugosa roses are all frost-hardy and the species are freeze-hardy also. As well, the following list contains hybrids selected for their capacity to withstand the hard frosts and winter-frozen soils of the mid-western states of the USA and Canada without special protection.

- **'Applejack'** *1973 – clear pink, semi-double blooms; wonderful fruity, apple-scented flowers and stout upright growth that makes a good bushy plant about 1.5m (5ft) tall or more. Flowers are produced repeatedly.*

- **'Country Dancer'** *1973 – rather blowzy and fancy-free double flowers of rich pink; a simple beauty with inbuilt reliability, healthy growth, tidy habits, to 1.5m (5ft) and with repeated bursts of bloom until frosts come.*

- **'Henry Hudson'** *1976 – a humdinger and one tough rose! Rich green leaves that set off to perfection beautifully formed ruffled, semi-double flowers of pure white with a centre of golden stamens. The buds are round and deep pink on the outside, the colour carrying over into the open flowers as a hint of pale blush when the weather is cool. To add to the beauty, the flowers are clove-scented.*

- **'Honeysweet'** *1984 – lovely soft apricot flowers on a compact bush about 1m (3ft) high. Nose-tingling honey-sweet perfume and good follow-on blooming throughout the warm months.*

- **'Jens Munk'** *1974 – the bright, pink semi-double blooms with a twist in the centremost petals remind one of the silken blooms of a tree peony, scaled down to rose size. The boss of bright gold stamens and warm, spicy perfume enhances the pleasure of this lovely rose. Within a few years of planting, the bush will grow into a dome-shaped shrub about 1.5m (5ft) high and the same in width.*

- **'Les Sjulin'** *1981 – a terrific perfume that harks back to the heavily fragrant roses of the 19th century. And that's not all; its flowers are big, semi-doubles, a blend of coral pink and light rose-red that appear all through summer on a handsome bushy plant.*

- **'Louis Jolliet'** *1991 – almost a climber and thus suitable for growing on rustic wooden tripods, fences and verandah posts. Great spicy perfume from double blooms that are continuously on show from early summer into autumn. Attains a height of about 3m (10ft).*

- **'Martin Frobisher'** *1968 – a tall and imposing shrub to 3m (10ft) or so, which is erect and slightly spreading. Grey-green leaves are a perfect foil for pale, flesh-coloured, fully-double flowers that are almost white at the outer edges and a shade or two darker at their hearts. Continuously in bloom all summer; sweetly scented and utterly hardy in mild dry areas and in the coldest zones. A marvellous plant that deserves to be more widely used.*

Subtropical climates, with their steamy days and warm nights, are not ideal for rose growing but there are varieties which are suitable for these conditions, such as Rosa chinensis 'Mutabilis' (below).

HEAT-TOLERANT ROSES

Choices for the subtropics

- **'Comtesse du Cayla'** *1902* – *a hybrid of* Rosa chinensis *'Mutabilis' with loose, semi-double flowers that open as pale buff-yellow and develop rich, apricot and rose-pink shades before finally turning dark wine-red. Masses of flowers on a vigorous shrub to about 3m (10ft).*

- **'Duchesse de Brabant'** *1857* – *a popular rose dating from 1857 and still found growing in many old gardens. Incurved semi-double flowers have been likened to sea shells. Small clusters of moderate-sized flowers in delicate shades of pearly pink, cream and white. Grows to about 2.5m (8ft) and just as wide. Attractive as a hedging plant.*

- **'Le Vésuve'** *1825* – *low, open growth to about 2m (6ft) with dark foliage and a continuous display of semi-double blooms carried in spreading "candelabras" of buds and flowers. Each bloom is a blend of pale pink that darkens as the outer petals age to a deep rose-pink.*

- **'Madame Charles'** *1864* – *while each flower is small, there are many flowers over a long season, and they are borne in large, airy clusters. Spreading growth to about 3m (10ft). The semi-double flowers are pale cream-pink inside; the outer petals "scroll" back to show a deep rose-pink on their under-side. A charming effect and an elegant flower.*

- **'Mamam Cochet'** *1893* – *a rather awkward, angular habit of growth, but with such glorious flowers that this is forgiven; high-centred and pointed, packed with petals, strongly scented and a delicious combination of two shades of pink smudged with cream. Strong, healthy growth, dark foliage and about 2m (6ft) high.*

- **'Parsons Pink China'** *(also known as* **'Old Blush'**) *1789* – *an ancient China rose, it has charming flowers which are silvery pink with a darker flush. The large clusters of semi-double flowers are almost continuously blooming. A moderately strong shrub rose with upright growth to about 1m (3ft) high. Strongly scented.*

- **Rosa chinensis 'Mutabilis'** *1934* – *dense, twiggy growth that mounds up so that by seven years or so it can make a large shrub about 3m (10ft) all round; it can be pruned smaller. Continuous display of flowers from small clusters of buds that at first open pale apricot and then develop as the bloom ages into rose-pink and finally, deep pink.*

- **'Safrano'** *1839* – *a semi-single, soft, old-gold coloured flower that has charmed gardeners since the days of the gold rush in California and Australia. The bush is low and spreading – about 2m (6ft) tall and wide, and the leaves are a rich dark green, tinged with red. The flowers are carried continuously in large, airy clusters.*

WILD ROSES

An everlasting passion

In many parts of the world roses can be found, apparently growing wild. They're often seen in neglected gardens, around historic settlements or in old, overgrown cemeteries. In their exuberant, tangled masses they seem healthy and strong and they flower beautifully year after year, even when left to fend for themselves.

Yet these are not always true wild roses; they are in many cases improved forms, originally brought in from the wild by keen-eyed enthusiasts. Over the years, as even better forms developed from seedlings, they too would have been planted in gardens, their strength and beauty endearing them to succeeding generations.

Origins of the Species

The truly wild roses are found away from the settlements and cultivated gardens. They are found in the hedgerows of fields and along the sunny edges of woodlands, among the sand dunes of the moors and coast, and in the open grasslands of the northern hemisphere.

In nature, roses are found from the Kamchatka Peninsula of western Siberia down to Baja California in Mexico. Others are found in the semi-deserts of Turkey, Iran, Iraq, Afghanistan and into the misty Himalayan foothills of northern India and Nepal. More still flourish in the lush semi-tropical climate of southern China.

A world of wild roses

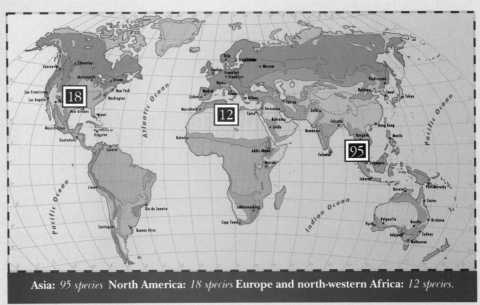

Asia: *95 species* **North America:** *18 species* **Europe and north-western Africa:** *12 species.*

Rosa filipes 'Kiftsgate', a spectacular rose capable of reaching 30m (100ft), bursts into bloom, outshining all the other plants in this expansive, colourful garden.

SUMMARY OF WILD SHAPES

The four growth habits

All wild roses are woody shrubs that form a light framework of trunks and branches which may be twiggy and dense, or stout and very open.

In some species, the growth is very long and rambling, as in *Rosa wichuraiana* **from Japan.**

In others, it scrambles high into trees with the aid of large hooked thorns, as in *Rosa gigantea* **from southern China.**

Some species spread outwards by vigorous suckers; *Rosa gallica* **and its family is one such group.**

Others, such as *Rosa setigera*, **have branches which take root wherever they touch the ground.**

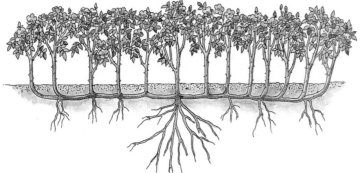

The abundant, single white flowers of Rosa longicuspis are impressive cascading over a gateway, but, be warned, this hardy, very vigorous rose can reach about 24m (80ft). Birds love its oval, orange-red hips and their scattering of seeds can present problems – more roses than first planned.

This very wide distribution, across many different climatic zones, suggests that roses are very adaptable plants. And so they are. Today, there are roses for a wide range of garden conditions.

More than 100 Natural Species

Altogether there are about 125 kinds of wild rose. Each kind is called a species because it is distinctly different from all others .

Most wild roses are found in Asia where approximately 95 species occur. About 18 come from North America and the rest, about 12 species, are native to Europe and north-western Africa. No species roses are found growing naturally in the southern hemisphere; southernmost, they are found in southern India, the Philippines, Morocco and Eritrea. Such tropical and subtropical wild roses are rarely grown in cultivated gardens. They include species such as *Rosa gigantea* which is too big for most gardens, and some scrubby, scruffy members of the *R. pimpinellifolia* clan.

Using the Natural Species
Their wild wonderful ways

Wild roses come in an amazing range of shapes and sizes. *Rosa filipes* 'Kiftsgate', for instance is a climber that develops into a huge plant; very old plants have been measured at over 30m (100ft) high with a spread of 40m (130ft) and more. In comparison, *R. chinensis* is a modest, twiggy bush which might reach about 3m (10ft) with a spread of 1.5m (5ft). Even smaller and more compact is *R. spinosissima* from Europe which spreads widely by suckers in sandy, barren soils but rarely grows much over 1m (3ft) tall.

Some other varieties also spread over enormous distances and, with their dense foliage and heavy branching make excellent weed-smothering ground cover. *R. horrida* is one such rose. It has many short, stout thorns which provide the added bonus of deterring intruders.

On page 26 we show you how to make use of wild roses in your own garden – as climbers, as

Rosa gallica officinalis

Rosa villosa **'Duplex'**

Rosa cinnamomea **'Plena'**

screening shrubs, as hedges and barriers, as groundcovers and for erosion control. Their beauty and versatility will astound you.

Flowers: Singles and Doubles

All natural species normally produce simple, single flowers; that is, one row of just five petals. But mutations do occur. Sometimes the difference will be in the flowers; they may be bigger, or a different colour, or they may have semi-double or fully-double flowers.

Double-flowered forms of wild roses have long been valued and, over the centuries, breeders have used them to produce flowers with increasing numbers of petals. Today the typical rose flower has multiple rows of petals in a voluptuous blossom. But the single flowers of the wild species have a simple beauty that still appeals to many gardeners.

The flowers of natural species commonly occur in shades of pink, but there are also a good many white-flowered species, quite a few shades of mauve, a clutch of clear yellows, some creams and some fine bright reds.

Rosa moyseii **produces small clusters of large, bottle-shaped hips.**

Rosa rugosa **has hips that are about the size of small apples.**

The small clusters of dull, dark fruit on *Rosa spinosissima.*

Don Brice (top far left) / Rodney Hyett (top centre & right) / Photos Horticultural (bottom left & right)

Hips

Providing colour for the winter months

Underneath the petals is the seed pod. In roses this is called a 'hip' or 'hep'. After pollination by a flying insect, the petals fall and the hip swells as the seeds develop inside it. In autumn it ripens from green to shades of orange, red, rusty brown or even black. Eventually, the seed is dispersed, most often by birds.

The hips are colourful and shapely. Some are round and fat and carried in large bunches, as in *Rosa virginiana* – in this case the hips are bright red and very shiny. *R.* x 'Dupontii' produces big, airy clusters of small, orange hips; all the many forms of the Scots Rose, *R. spinosissima* have small clusters of round, dull black fruits.

R. moyesii, *R. davidii* and many other Chinese species produce small clusters of large bottle-shaped hips of red or orange. *R. pisocarpa* and *R. farreri* produce tiny versions of the same shape. Rugosa roses are valued as much for their fruits the size of small apples as their rugged dark green leaves and silken flowers.

Leaves

Subtle colours and textures

The leaves of modern roses don't attract much attention – they're a dark, red-green and almost round with a blunt point. But it's a different story with their ancestors. Wild roses offer a selection of leaf shapes, sizes and colours in textured or smooth finishes.

The leaves of roses are always arranged in pairs of leaflets along a central stem with one leaf at the outward end at the apex. A few roses may show only three leaflets, but five or seven is more common and many species roses have nine leaflets. Most rose leaves are smooth; they may be glossy or dull, and some are plum-red when new, while a few are covered in a silver "bloom" or powder.

The leaves of *Rosa rugosa* are large, rich green, and deeply veined, while those of *R. multiflora* 'Watsoniana' are narrow and smooth, not unlike the leaves of a weeping willow tree.

Rosa rugosa **'Fru Dagmar Hastrup' (top) has rugged, rich green leaves and silken flowers, while (above)** *Rosa multiflora* **'Watsoniana's' leaves are narrow and smooth.**

WILD
roses for today's
GARDENS

*Know them before you
grow them*

I magine using a swimming pool surrounded by
roses that are too big. The long branches,
well-armed with strong thorns, reach out and
catch on towels and bare skin ... ouch!

Before selecting any kind of rose for planting
in your garden, be sure to know what it will grow
into and that its ultimate size and shape will suit
the proposed location. A rampageous climber, for
example, cannot be tamed by pruning to fit into
a modest suburban garden; it will grow as its
ancestors have always grown and, if it is not
allowed to swamp all surrounding plants and
buildings with abundant, vigorous growth, it
may die as a result of yearly attempts to prune it
into submission.

'Lady Banks Rose' (*Rosa banksiae* 'Lutea') and
its white form will always be big plants. Roses that
are large shrubs will always grow that way; no
amount of pruning will convince them to become
small bushes.

Read descriptions carefully before you buy any
rose, and especially those concerning natural
species. Be warned, the information on nursery
labels is often sketchy so, if necessary, look up your
choice in a specialist rose book or the descriptive
catalogue of a rose growing nursery.

*A large shrub which grows to about 7m (20ft), Rosa
banksiae alba plena produces small, rosette-like
double white flowers which look superb trailing over
a structure, such as this arch.*

Jaime Plaza

GROWING WILD ROSES

Tips for success

■ All roses need an open, sunny position, with at least 5 hours of direct sun each day.

■ Newly planted wild roses do not like competition from the roots of old, established trees and large shrubs. Plant them at a safe distance.

■ Roses do not flower well when they are overshadowed by large trees or buildings.

■ Roses can best resist diseases and pests if they grow where the breezes can stir the air around the plants.

■ With few exceptions, wild roses grow best in well-drained soils; bogs, swamps and sticky clay won't do.

■ Mulch heavily for good weed control and good moisture retention.

■ Watering in summer can be minimal; a soaking once every three or four weeks is usually ample.

■ Feeding wild roses is simple; mulch with compost, pea straw, stable litter and apply a ration of complete plant food in early spring.

■ Wild roses don't need pruning every year; just remove any dead branches and one or two of the oldest woody canes, so that the bush renews itself with some fresh, strong growth each year.

■ Wild roses blossom on wood that is one year old, so avoid pruning that cuts into this wood.

■ Pruning that is necessary is best done immediately after the flowers have finished in mid-summer so that the plant has time to grow new wood ready for the next flowering season.

■ Winter pruning is uncomfortable in cold, windy and wet climates and serves only to cut off the flowers to come in early summer.

■ Spraying for bugs and diseases is unnecessary for wild roses and their hybrids. Tough characters like Japanese beetles and earwigs may need attention, but with other flowering shrubs, such as perennials, groundcover plants and bulbs, these pests should not be the problem they are in rose-only gardens.

■ Try to see wild roses growing in a mature garden before making a final choice and placing an order.

■ Remember that the natural, characteristic habits of roses can never be altered by pruning; choose roses that will fit into the spaces available without persuasion by threats and chainsaws.

THE MOYESII CLAN

Among the best of all tall roses

osa moyesii and its forms – or roses which have a Moyesii as a parent – are tall arching shrubs with growth that will reach up to 5m (16ft). Even the smallest types reach 3m (10ft). The branches are covered in smooth, green-yellow bark that greys with age. There are comparatively few large, thin thorns and very few bristles. The single flowers (about 5cm (2in) in diameter), in various shades of red, are clustered on short stalks that appear along the year-old growth on the top one third of each branch. The foliage is ferny in appearance, but is also quite stout and usually light green in colour.

SELECTING WILD ROSES

Two wild clans

Not all wild roses are good choices for suburban gardens. Some are way too big, while others are not particularly decorative. However, there are two major clans of related roses and a few other individual species with a lot to offer gardeners. These two, Moyesii and Rugosa, are outlined on the following pages.

Long Display

The bushes are deciduous and, when bare, you can clearly see the "vase" shape of the plants. The basal branches are strong enough to support light climbers, such as *Clematis viticella* or *C. campanulata*, which give two seasons of flower interest in spring and summer, as well as a stunning display of large bottle-shaped hips from late summer until the end of autumn – if the birds don't get them first. The hips are also long lasting when picked for indoors.

Easily Grown

Rosa moyesii and its near relatives and hybrids need deep soils to perform at their best. They are easily grown from seed, and the seedlings should flower within three years. All Moyesii roses sucker on very short underground stems that stay close to the parent plant so that they form a compact cluster of branches.

Why Select Moyesii Roses?

They are the fireworks rose. The tall shrubs are arched over at the top, making a spreading crown of canes and ferny foliage. In late spring the crown is liberally spangled with gorgeous scarlet, crimson or pink flowers. From late summer until the end of autum, Moyesii roses produce a stunning display of hips in drooping clusters all along the branches. Of all roses these must surely be the crown jewels.

Pick of the bunch

- **'Arthur Hillier'** – *grows to about 3m (10ft) with a spreading crown. Flowers are carried in small clusters and are an eye-catching deep pink with just a hint of purple. The flowers are followed by large hips which turn vibrant orange shades in autumn.*

- **Rosa glauca** – *has a long history as a favourite shrub of carefree gardeners. The moderate growth to 3m (10ft) has dark red-brown bark and plum-coloured leaves overlaid with a fine silver bloom. The small, bright pink-red flowers with paler centres are carried in open clusters. From these flowers, small, round, dark red hips develop in autumn. A handsome rose, it is "big" in leaf colour and impact, especially when teamed with other silver-leafed plants.*

- **Rosa sweginzowii** – *a close relative of Rosa. moyesii but far more prolific in the quantities of hips produced. Flowers are deep pink, about 5cm (2in) across and carried in clusters of three to eight along the length of the long arching canes. The smooth, wine-bottle hips ripen to a dusky red-brown. A first-class shrub rose, it grows to about 3m (10ft) tall with a spread of around 2m (6ft).*

- **Rosa virginiana** *is a native of the east coast of North America and will grow in damp, sunny positions as well as more well-drained soils. However, grown in a damp place on its own roots, it will sucker widely. Generally no more than 1.5m (5ft) tall and about 2m (6ft) across, this dome-shaped shrub has rich green, glossy foliage that covers the bush. From a good display of musk pink single flowers, a brilliant crop of glossy bright red hips develop. A luxurious plant.*

- **Rosa willmottiae** – *single mauve-pink flowers which always manage to look rather delicate and waifish. Scattered thickly over the tall growth, the flowers have a carefree air that endears them to me every year. Perhaps the tallest of the group, **R. willmottiae** makes a terrific background shrub where its height usefully carries a pink colour theme to 4m (13ft) or so, especially if there is some support from nearby shrubs or small trees.*

*Rosa glauca **has small flowers but is "big" in impact.***

THE RUGOSA CLAN

Strong, stout and very useful

Rosa rugosa and its many forms are frequently found doing service in tough environments. Originally from the sandy dunes around the shores and islands of the northern Pacific, these hardy, resilient roses were introduced from the wild by the Japanese before the days of Westernisation.

Valued for their rugged, dark green leaves, silken flowers and big, colourful hips, Rugosas were quickly procured by Western horticulturists and have been hybridised and planted extensively since.

Rosa rugosa 'Fru Dagmar Hastrup'

Rosa rugosa 'Rubra'

What You Can Expect

The Rugosa roses make broad, spreading shrubs covered with heavy foliage which reaches to the ground. The stems and branches, which are supple while being strong and stout, are covered with a dense, fawn-coloured felting which is liberally spiked with thin spines. The leaves are dark green and deeply veined, and the petals have a very attractive silken sheen which sets them apart from other roses. In autumn the foliage of many Rugosas turns yellow. At the centre of each flower is a boss of cream stamens which contrasts with the pink and cerise-coloured flowers and blend well with the white-flowered kinds.

Many Uses

Rugosas make wonderful low, unclipped hedges, and for mass planting they make an effective groundcover. This kind of planting looks very good over a large area.

Individual plants work well as specimens set among rocks and pebbles, or in the foreground of banks of shrubs and screens. Set against the silver-grey wood of an old post-and-rail fence, the silken flowers, dark foliage and compact growth are breathtaking.

Easy Care

Like all wild roses, Rugosas need no annual pruning and no spraying. Just cut away the dead branches from the underside of the shrubs every few years.

All roses perform best when they have fair soil, good mulching and light feeding, and occasional deep watering in hot, dry months. Yet Rugosas are extremely cold-hardy and have been used to breed roses suited to the Canadian and central United States winters.

Stirling Macoboy (bottom left) / Don Brice (top left) / Leigh Clapp (right)

Pick of the bunch

- **'Calocarpa'** – *this is a hybrid form of Rosa rugosa. The big flowers are a soft shade of pink with definite magenta tones. The developing buds are long, slender and elegant. Some people claim it reblooms but, in my experience, it has not. The prolific crop of hips is scarlet-orange. About 2m (6ft) tall.*

- **'Corylus'** – *another hybrid of Rosa rugosa. The bush is smaller than many Rugosas, and the leaflets are narrower. The bush grows to 1.5m (5ft), and is dome-shaped and densely twiggy. The flowers are a silvery, medium pink, single and well-perfumed. A colourful crop of scarlet hips follows.*

- **'Delicata'** – *a very pretty rose with two or three rows of crepe-textured, lilac-pink petals. The flowers have a charming informality with petals unevenly disposed and displayed. At the centre of each flower is a mass of cream-yellow stamens. Typical Rugosa hips, growth and leaves, and the bonus of some rebloom all summer and into autumn.*

- **'Fru Dagmar Hastrup'** – *this charming, low, compact bush with a spreading growth (1.5m [5ft] high and wide) has a good cover of dark green leaves, and wonderful pale pink single flowers in small clusters, or singly, over a long season. By early summer the first crop of flowers is maturing into big red hips that intermingle with the later flowers – a lovely sight that invites all sorts of other plantings to complement its blooms and fruit.*

- **'Rubra'** *(syn. 'Atropurpurea')* – *similar to the most common wild forms, this compact, rounded shrub produces masses of big, cerise-red flowers with a fine silky finish. These are followed by big, bright red hips. Like the white form above, this plant has a long flowering season.*

- **'Scabrosa'** – *very popular since its introduction in 1950, for it has all the good qualities of Rugosas. The leaves and flowers are extra big, the scarlet hips positively enormous. Growth is vigorous too – around 2m (6ft), but not ungainly or straggly. Excellent for informal hedges, it has an outstanding appearance that enables it to stand alone as a specimen by a gate or at the end of a border.*

Rosa rugosa 'Scabrosa'

A Garden of
WILD ROSES

Here are eight wild shrub roses, mostly with tall growth, 2-4m (6-13ft), that could form the backbone of a pretty pink garden. Interplanted with pink or white flowered kiss-me-quick (*Centranthus ruber*), pink and white daisies and your choice of other perennials and annuals in the same colour grouping, the effect would be charming. Our plan would take a minimum space of 12 x 5m (40 x 16ft). Use fewer roses for a smaller area.

In The Pink

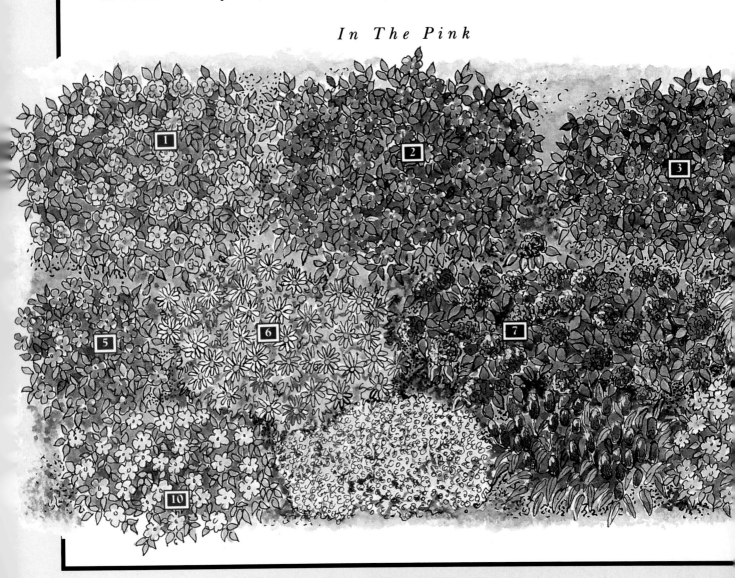

KEY FOR PLAN

1	R. californica 'Plena'	**8**	Bronze fennel
2	R. scabrosa	**9**	R. corylus
3	R. villosa 'Duplex'	**10**	3rd row: 'Fru Dagmar Hastrup'
4	R. delicata		
5	2nd row: R. calocarpa		
6	Daisies		
7	R. centranthus 'Kiss Me Quick'		

Rosa roxburghii 'Plena'

Leigh Clapp

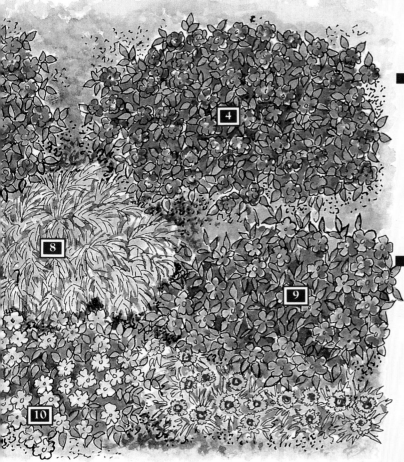

DOUBLE WILD ROSES

Pick of the bunch

The forms of wild roses which have mutated naturally to produce double and semi-double flowers have a long association with our gardens. Collected from the wild aeons ago, they have been grown for centuries.

■ ***Rosa californica* 'Plena'** – *tall, somewhat arching growth to 3m (10ft) and delicate ferny foliage make a lovely background for the clusters of charming semi-double, spicy pink flowers with paler flesh colours near their outer edges. Perfume is particularly lovely, and the flowers rival the "Sweetheart Rose" ('Cecile Brunner').*

■ ***Rosa villosa* 'Duplex'** - *sometimes called 'Wolley Dodd's Rose' after an English parson in whose garden it was found. This is a big shrub that will grow 3 to 4m (10-13ft) tall with strong grey-barked canes and over-arching top growth. The large leaves are downy and silvered with grey, making quite a handsome bush. The flowers have about three rows of slightly waved, soft pink petals, but there is only one flush of blooming early summer. Some hips are set and these are big, bristly, glossy and bright red. Also known as R. pomifera 'Duplex'.*

■ ***Rosa roxburghii* 'Plena'** – *in contrast to R. villosa 'Duplex', this rose is low, broad and dense in its habits. The foliage is mid-green and smooth. There are few thorns on the 1.5 x 2m (5 x 6ft) shrub but they are needle-like and painfully sharp. The low, spreading growth and pink flowers blend beautifully with tough Mediterranean shrubs, especially the new pink-flowered Rosemary and any of the pink-or white-flowered Cistus species. For foliage contrast, add bronze fennel.*

■ ***Rosa majalis* 'Plena'** – *here is a tall (3.5m [12ft]) shrub rose ideal for background planting in any garden where pinks and mauves are being combined for an harmonious and delicate effect. The foliage is rather grey-green and unassuming; it mixes well with other shrubs and flowering plants. The small lilac-pink flowers dot the bush over four weeks or so in early summer. Any number of perennials associate well with this colour, creating a satisfying design which is easy to arrange and looks so professional.*

An "almost natural" hybrid, 'Complicata' has low spreading growth and big warm pink flowers in clusters. It forms a happy partnership here as a background for an 'Iceberg' and *Eschscholzia californica.*

'Complicata'

'Fruhlingsgold'

Don Brice (inset left & right)/ Rodney Hyett (top inset)/ Paddy Wales (left)

WILD HYBRIDS

From natural species to "almost natural" hybrids

With human nature being both peverse enough to try to improve on perfection and curious enough to try anything once, it was inevitable that rose growers would cross-breed one wild rose with another and then cross and recross the resulting progeny. Thus there are now hundreds of hybridised shrub roses that are closely related by their breeding to the wild roses of the world. They are just as hardy and, to many people, even lovelier looking. In selecting your varieties, it's best to see the plants as mature specimens in a garden, nursery or park but, failing that, consider these few tried and true favourites for your garden.

"ALMOST NATURAL" HYBRIDS

Pick of the bunch

■ **'Abbotswood'** – *has tall open growth to about 2m (6ft) high and arching outward at the crown to spread about the same distance across. Its pale green leaves have an astonishing apple scent which is especially noticeable after rain. The bright pink, semi-double flowers spangle the branches in late spring and are followed by decorative orange-red hips. Cold-hardy.*

■ **'Agnes'** – *is a hybrid of Rosa rugosa and 'Persian Yellow' (R. foetida 'Persiana') and carryies a great reputation for performing well in cold climates. The very double flowers are a soft yellow and have a distinct perfume. Flowers appear in profusion in early summer on a compact and upright bush that regrettably shows rather ugly thorny ankles under the canopy of leaves. This can be rectified by underplanting with a perennial, such as Geranium pratense. The foliage is deep green and heavily puckered. This plant is not recommended for warm climates, as the flowers fade to a bland off-white as soon as they open.*

■ **'Complicata'** – *a fine, free-flowering shrub with large light green leaves, low spreading growth and big warm pink single flowers displayed in small clusters. It flowers once only, in early summer. Plants grown in open conditions usually reach about 1.5m (5ft), and spread to about 2m (6ft). Few thorns on its supple canes.*

■ **'Fimbriata'** – *familiar to older gardeners as 'Dianthiflora' or 'Phoebes's Frilled Pink', this rose has flowers that are frilled like a small garden Pink (Dianthus). Almost white with pale pink tones when newly opened, the small flowers are sweetly scented and produce a few hips in autumn. Growth is upright to about 2m (6ft) with a dense bright green leaf cover that is disease resistant. A tough oldie from 1891, it is ideal for recreating the atmosphere of a cottage garden.*

■ **'Fruhlingsmorgen'** – *a tall, arching shrub with widely spaced leaves and a fearsome array of thorns. But having seen the flowers, most people become convinced that this is worth a place in the garden. The single flowers are a warm shade of pink paling to creamy white, and then gold near the centre of each bloom. A tuft of dark red stamens at the centre of each flower stands out against the paler background of petals. The name means "spring morning", and the colours reflect the sky at that time perfectly. A few hips are set and there are a few flowers for summer after the first main flush of blooms. Not as well-known as its sister, 'Fruhlingsgold', yet a spectacular specimen shrub.*

'Fruhlingsmorgen'

■ **'Nevada'** – *has among the largest flowers of any shrub rose. They are graceful, delicate and a fine creamy white that is easy to incorporate into a garden plan. The arching growth has very few thorns and makes a broad mounded shrub about 2m (6ft) high and as much across. The leaf cover is ample, although not dense. Each leaf is grey-green with some red tints along the edges; a colour that is repeated in the bark of young stems and twigs. There is no perfume and no hips.*

Nature's Glorious
YELLOW ROSES

Rosa x 'Cantabrigiensis'.

While many natural species occur in shades of pink there are yet others which come in a treasure trove of clear yellows from the softest cream to the richest chrome. Before the mid-19th century there were no hybrid yellow roses. The only yellow roses available to relieve the sea of pink and red in rose gardens were either a few wild yellow roses or their very rare double forms. Today we have many modern hybrid yellow roses but the wild yellows and their close hybrids still offer exciting possibilities. Combining these roses presents an opportunity to make an outstanding garden that is at once both simple and elegant.

Rosa foetida 'Persiana'.

A Sunny Garden Theme

By planting yellow species roses and their close relatives in banks or groves, the foundation is laid for further development of the sunny theme. Simply planted among grass they will look stunning; imagine them paired with Golden broom, Cootamundra wattle, Pineapple broom or other yellow flowered shrubs. Yellow foliage plants could be included too, but be careful about where they are planted for most plants in this group bleach and burn badly given the sunny positions that wild roses need.

'Golden Chersonese'.

Photos Horticultural (top) / Leigh Clapp (centre) / Rodney Hyett (bottom)

Rosa foetida

Rosa foetida 'Lutea'.

'Canary Bird'

Pick of the bunch

■ **'Albert Edwards'** – to my eyes this is more cream than yellow but such variations add always desirable subtlety to a garden. Arching growth to 3m (10ft) and more gives impact without brashness. The flowers are single, slightly cupped and borne profusely for three to four weeks in late spring.

■ **'Canary Bird'** – a splendid tall, open shrub with elegant curving canes that can reach 3m (10ft) upwards before arching over to make a canopy of leaves and flowers of about the same width. Growth can be less in hard soils and harsh climates, but wherever it grows, it can be relied on for a spectacular show of single soft yellow flowers with a slight musky scent. Only one season of flower and few hips, if any, but always a delight in late spring. It is a selected garden form of the Chinese species Rosa xanthina.

■ **'Golden Chersonese'** – a larger growing hybrid of Rosa ecae and so prolific that the blooms smother the branches when the shrub flowers in early summer. Blossoms are single, clear yellow and emit a subtle, spicy perfume. The dense, twiggy growth is an improvement on its parents and makes a bush about 2m (6ft) tall and almost as wide. Only one season of bloom, but oh boy!

■ ***Rosa hugonis*** – known widely in America as 'Father Hugo's Rose' after a missionary in China who was a keen amateur botanist and plant collector. A graceful bush, it grows upward on dark brown canes and spreads outward at the crown into gently arching growth lightly clothed with dark green ferny foliage. Soft butter-yellow flowers are plentifully scattered on the branches in late spring. It grows to about 1m (3ft) high and about 1.5m (5ft) across.

■ ***Rosa ecae*** – a very open, wiry bush with tiny dark green ferny leaves and rich brown stems and thorns. It grows to about 2m (6ft) and bursts into bloom in late spring. Tiny, brilliant chrome-yellow flowers are liberally spangled along the branches. The season lasts only for about three weeks, but such is their impact that it is well worth inclusion. The Afghanistan home of this rose indicates its extreme hardiness in barren soils and harsh climates.

■ ***Rosa foetida*** – another open bush to 2m (6ft) high, but with stouter branches than R. ecae and with larger leaves and much larger flowers. The single season of clear yellow flowers lasts for a few weeks. This species comes from Iran and is quite hardy in regard to cold and drought. Few hips are set, but what matter? They would only upset the all-gold colour scheme! R. foetida 'Persiana' is a fine semi-double form that adds to the party atmosphere.

■ ***Rosa x 'Cantabrigiensis'*** – is a vigorous but still charming rose with fine, ferny leaves, dark rusty red-brown stems and profuse pale cream-yellow single flowers along the branches.

LARGE-FLOWERED BUSH ROSES

Developed for exhibition

ention roses and most people think of plump, pointy buds which open into big, many-petalled flowers on stiff, upright bushes. Bush roses with large flowers have been popular since the last century and have been developed from 19th century roses, such as Bourbons, Hybrid Perpetuals, and Tea roses into Hybrid Teas, and the Grandifloras, of 20th century breeders.

While growth characteristics vary between varieties, they are all bush roses that grow to about 1.5m (5ft) high and the same width. Growth tends to be upright with the foliage concentrated at the crown of the plant and a show of stiff, naked branches clothed with strong thorns underneath. The flowers are large, about 15cm in diameter, and are carried on single stems or in small clusters of about three.

Brent Wilson

The beautiful, pure white blooms of 'Frau Karl Druschki', also known as 'Snow Queen', have earned this rose notoriety since its 1901 introduction.

Harmony reigns in a cottage-style garden where 'New Dawn', a delightful large-flowered climber, has spread to cover the chimney.

Thousands of Varieties

Developed for exhibition

The large-flowered bush roses have been developed mainly as flowers for exhibition in rose shows and for use in formal public rose gardens. While both these formative influences are no longer as popular as they were in the early years of the 20th century, they still exert a profound influence on the way we garden with roses. There are many thousands of varieties, all the work of hybridists. All the roses mentioned in this book from this point on are hybrids – the result of breeding programmes. We have separated them into two groups; large-flowered bush roses and modern shrub roses.

Choosing Large-Flowered Roses

How will you use them?

The individual blooms of large-flowered roses are exceptionally beautiful, but the bushes themselves are not always so pleasing. Often gardeners select a new variety for their gardens on the basis of the cut flowers on display at a rose show, only to find that the plant itself is a disappointment. Sometimes the bush is not only scrawny but the desired flowers are few and far between. The extraordinarily coloured 'Julia's Rose' is a case in point. Its few stunning blooms do not make up for an ungainly bush with poor foliage and spindly growth. A rose must do better than that to find a place in most gardens.

The opposite is just as bad. 'Queen Elizabeth' for example is a bush that grows monstrously huge, showing ugly, thorny ankles and shanks under a great dollop of leaves. True, its flowers are glorious, but they're held so high only the birds can see them. This sort of bush makes a marvellous tall hedge so long as frontline plants screen the nakedness of its lower limbs. Otherwise it has very limited use.

See Beyond the Blooms

Fascination with actual blooms should be tempered with a clear-headed appraisal of the bushes; the form of the bush, the health and colour of the leaves, and the number of flowers produced should complement the beauty and perfume of individual blossoms. Roses chosen for their good looks and fine flowers are often better in the landscape than those chosen for their flowers alone.

Designing with Bush Roses

Keep it simple

Any of the large-flowered bush roses can be included in the design of a small garden and can play a special role without taking over the whole site. Practising restraint is difficult, especially when faced with so many enticing choices, but if you want a garden design that works it is essential to control the urge to have one of everything.

With roses, this tendency can lead to a jumble of wildly clashing colours on bushes of all sizes and habit. Let harmony reign, let unity and serenity rule. Never buy one of every rose, or indeed of anything else, unless you have a very clear idea of how you are going to manage all those colours.

Even if you want nothing but roses, your rose garden will still look better if it is not made up of hundreds of different colours all mixed in together.

Decide on a Colour Scheme

And then stick to it

If your garden is not yet planted, decide on a colour scheme first. Keep this simple, i.e., have shades of the one colour only, or two colours that complement each other. In a small garden that's probably enough; the bigger the space the more colours you can introduce.

Let the colours be those that you like and that you know will go well together. With roses you've virtually every colour to choose from except blue and green, so you can create every combination from soft pastels to strong, bright primaries.

There are no rules – colour combinations don't have to be complementary to succeed, but if you are inclined towards planting a striking combination, think it through thoroughly, and then stick to it.

Four 'Grüss an Aachen' standards, a hedge of Lonicera nitida aurea and vibrant Nepeta cataria combine to create a formal effect; the stone column with flower-filled urn atop (one of two) echoes the formality.

CONSIDER A FORMAL GARDEN

Large-flowered bush roses lend themselves well to a formal garden design, their general habits of growth being either upright and stiff, or spreading and angular. These characteristics are not easily blended into an informal or "natural" style of garden of shrubs and mixed flowers, such as perennials, annuals and bulbs. As a rule, large-flowered bush roses do not enjoy close root competition from other plants and would be more susceptible to the diseases black spot and powdery mildew in the still air of a dense shrubbery. In a flower border, rose thorns will damage neighbouring plants and make life difficult for the gardener.

The ideal environment for accommodating these beautiful and very popular roses is the formal rose garden. It can be any size for which you have space; the bigger the area, the more elaborate can be the pattern made by beds and intersecting paths. But remember, the more beds you have in your rose garden, the more maintenance will be needed.

The smaller the space you have, the simpler the layout of the rose garden should be. In a tiny space, as few as four rose bushes can make a fine formal garden. I'd recommend a square or rectangular layout, since round gardens in small spaces leave too many left-over corners to fill.

A SMALL, FORMAL ROSE GARDEN

Creating formality in small spaces

One variety of rose ('Mrs B. R. Cant') has been used to suggest serenity in a small garden. An edging of boxwood hedging or dwarf lavender, clipped low to about 30cm (1ft) high, enhances the formal effect. Other plants, such as violets, Lamiums or lamb's tongues (Stachys lanata) may be added for additional colour and groundcover.

Ways to Create Formality

A square garden can have a pair of intersecting paths as the focal point of the design; a rectangular rose garden immediately suggests the possibility of a central pathway with beds either side. A formal garden can have a row of standard roses (all of the same kind) along a fence line and bedded underneath with pansies. This layout was popular in the 1930s and can suit houses of that era. Or the garden can consist of four old-fashioned roses surrounded by unconfined lavender hedges in a farm garden. Again, it could comprise a squad of potted roses arrayed with military precision on a patio or terrace.

Two Styles of Gardens

Strictly formal or more relaxed

Such gardens can be strictly formal and highly manicured, or there can be a degree of freedom and casualness. In the former style, every plant is carefully positioned, then trained and trimmed to conform to an overall design. Usually, there's nothing but mulch beneath the roses. In the latter style, although there's a framework of regularity and repeated patterns of planting, a more relaxed, cottage style can be had by underplanting with a free mix of shallow-rooted perennials or small bulbs (for suggestions, see "Planting Companions" on page 49). If the plants chosen are lower than the rose bushes, their roots will not compete with rose bush roots.

There are places for both kinds of gardening. The former may be appropriate if you are trying to establish a feeling of chic elegance around an inner-city terrace house, whereas a more relaxed atmosphere may better suit an older-style home in the country or suburbs. The choice is yours; there's no right or wrong way – just ideas that can be overturned or used as you wish.

Strictly formal gardens call for low, clipped hedges enclosing the rose beds. You can use English or Japanese box, myrtle or small-leafed privet; each of which can be simply trimmed square. Such a low border will hide bare earth and lead the eye straight towards the roses. Alternatively, you can train and

Rodney Hyett

clip such plants into more complicated shapes, such as standardised "lollipop" balls or corkscrews of greenery. Remember, boxwood needs to be clipped once a year at the end of the growing season, once the new growth has ripened.

Neatly trimmed and trained hedges, the climbing roses 'Iceberg' and 'Lamarque' and compact bush roses, including 'Dainty Bess', all feature in a formal rose garden. Inset: An 'Iceberg' frames a section of this garden.

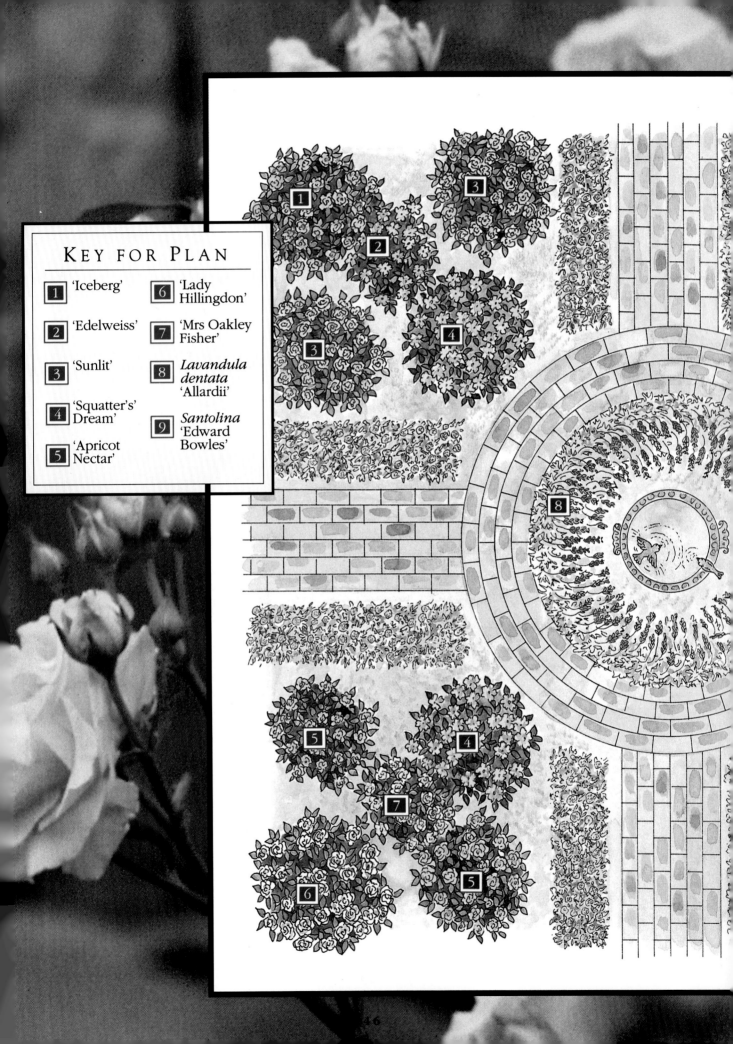

KEY FOR PLAN

1. 'Iceberg'
2. 'Edelweiss'
3. 'Sunlit'
4. 'Squatter's Dream'
5. 'Apricot Nectar'
6. 'Lady Hillingdon'
7. 'Mrs Oakley Fisher'
8. *Lavandula dentata* 'Allardii'
9. *Santolina* 'Edward Bowles'

A RONDEL FORMAL ROSE GARDEN

Creating elegance with a formal design

Gary Atchison (background) / Rodney Hyett (inset)

This formal, circular garden surrounds a birdbath standing on a plinth, and features a mix of roses, including 'Apricot Nectar' (above and background), in matching opposite garden beds. The rigid formality is softened by a billowing hedge of lavender around the bird bath and a low hedge of Santolina x 'Edward Bowles' bordering the paths. Groundcover can be achieved by planting violets.

In Small Gardens

Inspiration from roses

In small gardens a strongly European atmosphere can be be created by setting large pots of standard roses at regular intervals among a framework of low hedges and clipped topiaries.

Alternatively, a more relaxed formalism can be achieved with hedges of small shrubs which naturally attain compact, even shapes without regular, precise trimming. Small shrubs, such as the smaller growing lavenders and lavender cotton (*Santolina pinnata* 'Edward Bowles'), are particularly useful for planting along garden edges in this kind of design. Spent flowers should be sheared off, and an annual cut-back at the beginning of the growing season should be enough to keep such hedges within bounds.

Behind the hedges and under the rose bushes, shallow-rooted perennials or small bulbs can give extra colour that supports the scheme with complementary or contrasting tones. Plants chosen must be low, so that the formal look is not lost amid a tangle of growth. See "Planting Companions" at right.

Combining Colours

Remember, the simplest schemes are the best for gardeners who want to have some spare time for non-gardening activities. Keep colour combinations down to one or two tones that pick up the colours of the roses above them or of other nearby plants. Colour-blended seedlings of Violas and other annuals can work as a beginning to developing this idea of a unified colour scheme. Using annuals offers the chance to change the scheme each year, or more often as inspiration strikes.

A favourite rose that has withstood the test of time, 'Shot Silk', with its sheeny salmon-pink flowers, contrasts beautifully with mauve Clematis, 'Mrs P. T. James', surging side-by-side to enhance a country-style cottage.

Paddy Wales

PLANTING COMPANIONS

Easy-growers to team with roses

- **Annual flowers:** *Ageratum, alyssum, Californian poppy, candytuft, clove-scented pinks, Dianthus, Impatiens, lobelia, Nemophila, pansy, Petunia, Viola, Virginian stock.*
- **Perennial flowers:** *Anthemis, Armeria, low Campanula, catmint, Erigeron, Euphorbia robbiae, Festuca, Stachys, Stokesia, alyssum, violet.*
- **Herbs:** *Basil, chamomile, chives, garlic, marjoram, parsley.*
- **Bulbs:** *Algerian iris, Anemone nemorosa, Dwarf bearded iris, Freesia, Sparaxis.*

FORMAL ENTRANCE ROSE GARDEN

For a sunny townhouse

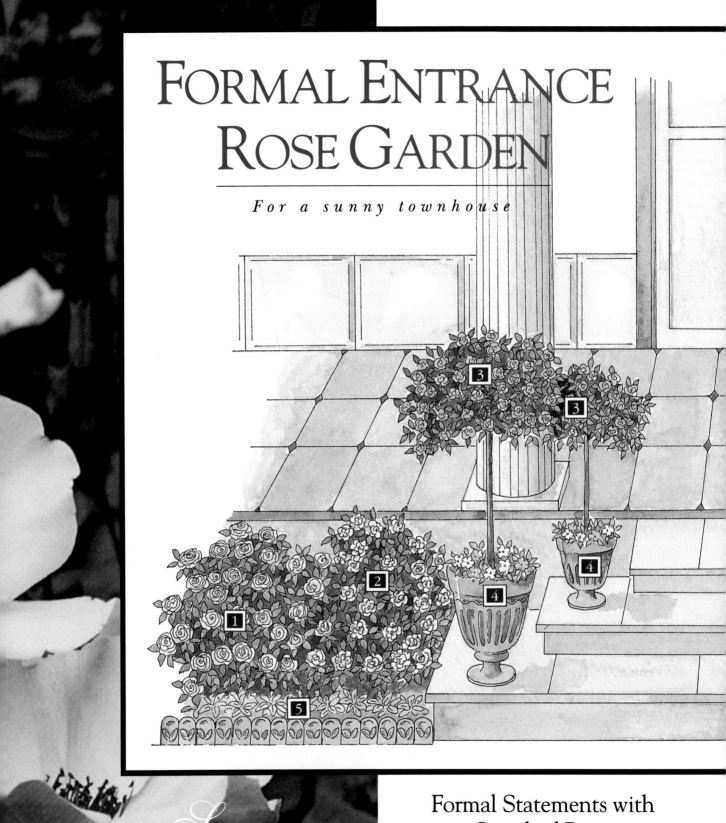

Simplicity rules in this elegant garden. The underplanting of Petunias for summer can be followed by white Impatiens hybrids for autumn. Background: 'Dainty Bess'.

Formal Statements with Standard Roses

The best formal effects are achieved with standard roses, that is, a rose grown on a single, straight, unbranched and leafless stem which is usually at least 1m (3ft) tall, but which may be taller. Standards have great visual impact, but it

KEY FOR
PLAN

1 'Grüss an
Aachen'

2 White 'Cecile
Brunner'

3 Standard 'Gold
Symphonie'

4 Yellow and
white Petunias

5 *Cerastium
tomentosum*

has to be said that the bushes need extra care in the form of regular pruning if their special shape is to be maintained.

Use standard roses to line paths or driveways, place one on either side of steps, gates or doors, or plant as a centrepiece to a circular bed. Generally, when using a number of standards, one colour only looks better than many different, randomly chosen colours. However, this isn't a rule. If you have an idea that involves more than one colour, try it. Be aware of the look you are creating and how it will combine with the rest of the garden. Remember, too, to allow standards room to spread, especially if you are planting them next to paths.

ROSES FOR STANDARDISATION

A selection of large-flowered standards

These roses produce compact growth that is well-suited for growing as a standard. I have included the dates of the roses' introduction to show that many great garden roses are not the hottest new releases but the tried stayers from yesteryear; their garden worthiness proven by time, and their fine qualities as much appreciated today as when they were first introduced.

- **'Chrysler Imperial'** *1952 – a favourite dark red with a strong, sweet perfume. Still one of the best with compact growth.*

- **'Comte de Chambord'** *1860 – much in demand with cottage gardeners and restoration enthusiasts. Rose-pink cupped and quartered, old-fashioned flowers. Good perfume, compact growth, light green leaves, thorny stems.*

- **'Comtesse Vandal'** *1932 – a classic rose with a rare, delicate quality that reappeared in catalogues after being unavailable for years. An old variety of bush rose that has regained popularity as it is thoroughly reliable. Elegant buds open to show a pinky-apricot high, centred flower.*

- **'Dame Edith Helen'** *1926 – large, cupped flowers with many silver-pink petals. The flower shape is old-fashioned with the petals tightly folded in on each other. The compact bush has the vigour and strength to carry the flowers perfectly.*

- **'Daydream'** *1925 – an Australian garden rose raised by Australia's foremost rose breeder, Alister Clark, and selected for its strong growth, hardiness and high flower production. Large heads of semi-double soft pink blooms are continuously produced over a long season. Unfazed by heatwaves.*

- **'Frau Karl Druschki'** *1901 – also known as 'Snow Queen' by some older gardeners. Pure white blooms are large and double, but without fragrance. It reblooms strongly after the first flush of summer.*

- **'Grandmère Jenny'** *1950 – a classic rose bred by the Meilland family in France. A rose that has all the good qualities of 'Peace', and much better growth and flower production. A graceful flower; soft yellow, peach and pink tones.*

- **'Grüss an Aachen'** *1909 – much like a modern cluster-flowered rose despite its date of introduction. The flower is loosely semi-double and a beautiful blend of palest pink, cream and pearl-white.*

- **'Michelle Meilland'** *1951 – another Meilland classic that has been overlooked in recent years, and with an appeal that beats a lot of more modern roses hands down. Similar to 'Grandmère Jenny', but with tones of colour that are more pinky cream. The flower form is very elegant.*

- **'Molly Sharman Crawford'** *1908 – a fine double white rose with beautiful buds that open to show a flower with rare refinement. The fully opened flowers hang down on their stems – a habit that can either be regarded as having old-fashioned charm or something to be avoided at all costs.*

- **'Mrs John Laing'** *1887 – full, fat and lovely, this old-timer has all the charm of yesteryear and continues to wow gardeners today. Strong perfume, plenty of rich pink flowers that last well, and strong growth.*

- **'Ophelia'** *1912 – one of the classic roses that has been revived by an increasingly discriminating marketplace. Elegant pointed buds open to show semi-double pale-pink flowers with just a hint of apricot. Growth to about 60cm (2ft).*

- **'Paul Neyron'** *1869 – similar to 'Mrs John Laing', but having an even more pronounced perfume and rich, dark pink flowers that are huge and globular. A fantastic rose. Growth to about 1m (3ft).*

- **'Permanent Wave'** *1932 – clusters of medium pink semi-double flowers that are ruffled along the petal edges produce a great show. Some scent.*

- **'Regensberg'** *(MACyou) 1980 – a white-centred, bright pink semi-double rose which blends into pale pink around the petal edges. Low compact growth and prolific blooming.*

- **'Spirit of Peace'** *(JACstine) 1994 – soft, honey colour with a hint of apricot, modern- style rose blooms with shapely buds and elegant open flowers. Masses of bloom over a long season and a telling spicy fragrance.*

Many Roses used as Standards

For glorious, weeping effects

Standard roses are made by grafting dormant growth buds of a selected rose variety onto a single, tall stem of a rose bred for the vigour of its root system and it's capacity to adapt to a wide range of soil conditions, drought and cold. Many standards are made by grafting climbing roses onto tall standards. These can look spectacular in a garden but they do require careful treatment to perform well. Careful staking, generous feeding and watering, and annual pruning are the rule to obtain good results.

Check carefully when buying standard roses that you are buying the right plant for the right situation: for formal gardens, where matching sets of standard roses are required, buy standard rose bushes; where a spectacular specimen plant is needed to stand alone in a lawn, a climbing rose grafted as a standard should be purchased – these are most often call "weeping standards".

Choosing a Standard Rose

Nurseries generally have very short lists of varieties grown as standards, but those that grow their own will often produce other varieties to order. As these take 12 months to grow to an appropriate size, advance ordering is essential. You will pay a little extra, naturally, but the outcome will be well worthwhile.

One of the all time great climbers, 'Crépuscule', (above) with its dense foliage and masses of gold and yellow flowers, looks superb grafted as a standard. Left: 'Paul Neyron'.

Also grown as a groundcover, the weeping, dark, glossy foliage and flesh-tinted white flowers of 'Sea Foam' perform beautifully as a standard. Inset: 'Chrysler Imperial'.

GROWING STANDARDS

Tips for success

■ *Standard roses must be staked carefully so they don't rock in the wind.*

■ *The standard stem must be tied securely, not tightly, to the stake.*

■ *Check the ties every month or so and re-tie as required.*

■ *Always remove any suckers that appear by exposing as much of the sucker as you can below ground level and pulling it out. Cutting suckers off at, or just below ground level, is a waste of time. Never try to poison them.*

■ *Feeding, as well as pest and disease control are essential for important plants such as these which are always the centre of attention.*

■ *Prune as for other large-flowered bush roses – the object being a fairly compact head of foliage and flowers at the top of the stem. This looks trim and formal and minimises the risk of wind damage to top-heavy growth.*

MINIATURES AS STANDARDS

Pick of the bunch

Many miniature roses are sold as dwarf standards, which make ideal potted plants. The best effects are achieved with varieties that are cascading in their habits of growth. Those mentioned below grow this way. Be on the lookout for others; new releases every year of miniature roses and small groundcover roses offer possibilities for creating lovely standards.

■ *'Pink Bells' (POUlbells)– neat, spreading growth that makes an ideal dwarf weeping standard of exceptional quality. The fully double flowers are a warm, spicy pink and each petal is quilled (i.e., rolled inwards along the edges). The display of flowers is prolific.*

■ *'Red Bells' (POUlred) – is similar, although a much darker shade of rose-red. There is also 'White Bells' (POUlwhite), although some believe it doesn't have the finesse and charm of 'Pink Bells'.*

■ *'Snow Carpet' – is quite different in form and utterly charming. Introduced as a miniature groundcover rose it has found its fame as a dwarf weeping standard. Smothered in tiny white flowers and glossy dark green leaves, it shows well against brickwork and stone and blends well with any number of other potted plants on a sunny terrace, by a doorway or flanking steps.*

■ *'Sweet Chariot' (MORchari) – with rich wine-purple flowers in abundance, it is a welcome addition to the colour range, offering garden planners a new colour to work into their designs.*

■ *'Sea Foam' 1964 - most often seen as a top-heavy standard rose in trendy designer-gardens, it was introduced as a vigorous groundcover rose with mounding and cascading dark glossy foliage and flesh-tinted white flowers. Spreading growth to about 1.5m (5ft) x 2m (8ft).*

Rodney Hyett / Garden at Tara, Guildford, Vic. (left) / Leigh Clapp (inset)

A LESS FORMAL ROSE GARDEN

Roses and daisies along a path

A golden garden of roses and other flowers in apricot, cream, pale yellow and peach colours. Other low-growing bulbs, perennials or annuals could also be included. Background: 'Betty Prior'.

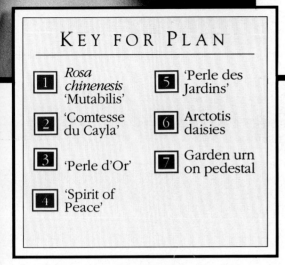

Stirling Macoboy (background)

SOFT BUT FORMAL

Rose gardens of the 1930s to 1950s

Standards have a grandeur and formality that suits both Victorian-era houses and modern imposing homes. However, for something less formal, consider using low bushes that grow to less than 1m (3ft). When one variety is massed or lined up, it can provide a carpet of colour that is relatively easy to maintain. This look suits the somewhat austere style of the double-fronted villas of the 1930s to 1950s. During this time, strict formalism associated with earlier Edwardian gardens had softened somewhat, but overall layouts were still usually geometric and based on the older patterns of the line and grid.

Massed Colour with Large-Flowered Bush Roses

Where compact growth is important

Many excellent roses, with fairly low, compact, bushy growth, can be used to develop bold colour masses within a formal pattern. To achieve solid blocks of colour that can be as modern as the rectangular primary colour compositions of painter, Piet Mondrian, or more subtle in complementary pastel shades, use only two or three colours and plant roses of the same kind for each colour. To avoid your garden looking like a public park, the garden beds could be edged with lavender cotton, dwarf lavender, or clumping perennials, such as pinks (Dianthus), Heuchera or black Mondo grass if you dare.

In these situations it is sensible to try to prune the roses to fairly uniform heights. Alternatively, in a less formal garden sheight can be added for visual interest by using taller background roses or roses grown on tripods or trellises. Where this is not possible, formal hedges punctuated with taller topiary pieces can achieve similar height variations without totally dominating the roses.

COMPACT LARGE-FLOWERED BUSH ROSES

Pick of the bunch

From all the thousands of bush roses that have been raised since the mid-19th century, the following is a selection of favourite compact varieties, i.e., less than about 1m (3ft) tall. Included, too, are a few climbers and other kinds that are well suited to creating a formal feeling in a garden.

■ **'Altissimo'** *(also known as* **'Altus'** *or* **'Sublimely Single')** *1966 – a stunning, almost single red, red rose of brilliant smouldering scarlet. The flowers are carried in clusters near the ends of canes. There is no other like it. However, growth tends to be sparse.*

■ **'Apricot Nectar'** *1965 – a fine, low bush with good leaf cover and small clusters of soft apricot flowers.*

■ **'Betty Prior'** *1935 – large clusters of carmine pink single blooms and good perfume. The compact bushes are covered with flowers all summer.*

■ **'Centenaire de Lourdes'** *(DELge) 1958 – large clusters of bright pink, semi-double flowers. The buds and open flowers are shapely. The bushes are covered in dark green leaves and there's a terrific display of orange, pear-shaped hips in autumn.*

■ **'Chanelle'** *1959 – soft, creamy apricot flowers are carried in large clusters on a low bushy plant and set off by glossy dark green leaves.*

■ **'Dainty Bess'** *1925 – a single rose with special charm. Soft pink flowers of five petals with dark red stamens. Simple and elegant, and a fine fragrance too.*

■ **'Dearest'** *1960 – a rose with all it takes to capture hearts! Sweetly fragrant, semi-double flowers of a lovely salmon-pink carried in large clusters on a compact, bushy plant.*

■ **'Edelweiss'** *(also known as* **'Snowline')** *1970 – beautiful cream, semi-single flowers borne in large clusters on low, compact growth that is well-clothed with foliage. Almost continuously flowering.*

■ **'Great News'** *1973 – an attractive blend of purple-violet shades with dark red foliage that adds to the exotic impact of this unusually coloured rose. A repeatedly blooming rose that is popular with flower arrangers for its distinctive colour.*

'Iceberg'

■ **'Gold Bunny'** *(MEIgronuri) (also known as* **'Gold Badge')** *1978 – clear golden yellow flowers; densely packed with petals and carried in large clusters. Mid-green leaves and bushy growth.*

■ **'Iceberg'** *(syn.* **'Schneewitchen')** *1968 – an extremely popular rose. Loosely semi-double flowers of pure white are borne in large clusters atop a bush well-covered with shiny light green leaves. Already a classic rose.*

■ **'New Dawn'** *1930 – a delightful climber with pale-pink, perfumed, semi-double flowers, which are grown singly or in clusters, and shiny, abundant foliage.*

■ **'Rosemary Rose'** *1954 – a fine, deep red rose with many petals packed old-fashioned style into each flower. Foliage is dark red-green and the compact bushes produce very big clusters of buds.*

■ **'Sexy Rexy'** *1984 (MACrexy) – not a name to charm everyone but don't be put off since the double, light salmon-pink flowers are exceptionally attractive. Compact growth with plenty of light green leaves.*

■ **'Shot Silk'** *1924 – a favourite rose that has withstood the test of time. Salmon-pink flowers with a satin sheen and a hint of yellow. The petals are held high in a globular flower form. Growth is bushy and upright and the foliage is a luxurious deep green.*

Leigh Clapp / Garden at Moidart (above) / Don Brice (right)

The solid blocks of glorious colour achieved with 'Great News' (front) and 'Gold Bunny' enliven a stately rose garden. Inset: 'Sexy Rexy'.

A country cottage is enhanced by the spectacular blooms of 'Archiduc Joseph' a hardy "tree" rose. Inset: 'Fragrant Cloud'.

Don Brice (left) / Stirling Macoboy (inset)

ROMANTIC, OLD-FASHIONED ROSE GARDEN

Instant age with "tree" roses

Another possibility exists for a retro-romantic style of formal garden. In this type of garden, big bush roses are minimally pruned so that they grow into a grove of tall shrubby rose "trees" which may reach 3m (10ft) or so in height. Low hedges of lavender or box outline the beds and groundcovering old-fashioned perennials, bulbs and annuals fill in the scheme, but the free-growing bushes complete the scene. Their size and exuberance adds the impression of maturity and can give new homes built in a 19th century-style the look of an authentic period garden quickly.

In old farm gardens and in time-worn cemeteries where they have not been pruned for decades, it's not unusual to find them 4m (13ft) tall and as wide.

Impressive Display

While it is possible to prune these bushes down to a more conventional size, I recommend allowing them to grow larger – the floral display is spectacular. Plants of this size add perspective and scale to a garden. They create a sense of drama and, of course, they can be underplanted with hardy perennials, bulbs, annuals and low-growing shrubs, such as scented-leaf Geraniums, Cistus and daisies. If your climate allows, light climbers, such as Clematis, can add a further season of colour with their showy flowers.

COUNTRY-STYLE FORMAL GARDEN

A rose garden among the lavender

Leigh Clapp (top) / Rodney Hyett (right) / Don Brice (below)

KEY FOR PLAN

1 'Monsieur Tillier'

2 'Old Blush'

3 *Murraya exotica*

4 'Cecile Brunner'

5 'Le Vésuve'

6 Hedge of lavender

TALL, LARGE-FLOWERED BUSH ROSES

A selection

Many of the following roses are very old, but do not be deterred by their age into thinking they must now be surpassed by new varieties; they are all guaranteed to be great "doers" with strong, healthy growth which may reach about 3m (10ft), and masses of flowers that just plead to be picked.

- **'Archiduc Joseph'** *1892 – very similar to 'Monsieur Tillier' in form, dimensions, foliage and colours, however 'Archiduc Joseph' has flowers with predominantly rose-pink shades, whereas 'Monsieur Tillier' has strong, copper-pink and apricot-pink tones as well as rose-pink. Both are lovely and very hardy.*

- **'Arillaga'** *1929 – a delicious combination of strawberry pink and cream subtly blended in a large old-fashioned looking flower. A strong plant.*

- **'Duchesse de Brabant'** *1857 – a refined rose which remains very popular today. Globe-shaped, semi-double flowers of palest pink with slight perfume and a season of flowers that goes on and on, especially in warm climates.*

- **'Fragrant Cloud'** *(also known as 'Duftwolke') 1967 – a modern rose compared with some listed here, but with qualities that will last; a pleasing scarlet red colour that is bright but not lurid, tall growth and a wonderful perfume.*

- **'Lady Hillingdon'** *1910 – still found in many old gardens where its tall, healthy growth, dark red-green leaves and glorious old gold flowers endear it to all. Long, elegant buds open to show a loose, semi-double flower that has some perfume. Flowers year-round in warm areas.*

'Duchesse de Brabant'

- **'Mrs Oakley Fisher'** *1921 – light and airy looking single flowers of soft old-gold colouring. The flowers are borne in large open clusters and set off by dark stems and leaves. Can take hard pruning but splendid when allowed to grow tall.*

- **'Maid of Honour'** *1986 – opens perfectly shaped buds to reveal a flower of rich, apricot tones that fades to a creamy apricot within a few days. The flowers are double and very fragrant. Not often found in lists and catalogues, but worth looking out for if you need this colour for your garden design.*

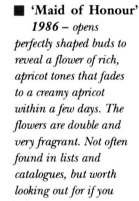
'Monsieur Tillier'

- **'Monsieur Tillier'** *1892 – a gem of rich pink, shading to soft apricot and old gold shades towards the centre of each petal-packed flower. Tall growth, dark red-green leaves and perfume too.*

- **'Mrs B. R. Cant'** *1901 – deep, globular, rich pink blooms that are paler towards the quartered centre petals. The flowers are large, well scented and carried over a long time. Very tall growth that almost qualifies this as a compact climber.*

- **'President Herbert Hoover'** *1930 – a vigorous, tall-growing rose with long, pointed*

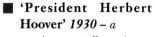
'Lady Hillingdon'

buds that reveal orange, deep rose-pink and buff flowers. Be sure to plant something pretty to hide his bare shanks.

- **'Squatter's Dream'** *1923 – raised at Bulla, near Melbourne, by Alister Clark and prized by him as a prolific garden rose bred to tolerate the heat and drought of the Australian summer. Large heads of single flowers that are a blend of copper, old gold and yellow set against dark green, glossy leaves. Growth is low and spreading. A good, continuous display of bloom all summer long.*

- **'Sunlit'** *1937 – an Australian-bred rose also raised by Alister Clark. Masses of large, semi-double old-gold flowers over a long season. As they mature, the flowers fade to a delicate apricot-cream colour. Low compact growth and a very healthy dark green foliage.*

- **'Tipsy Imperial Concubine'** *1982 – an ancient Chinese garden rose recently introduced to Western gardens. A fairly conventional old-fashioned style rose with flowers of palest cream tinged with pale pink.*

MODERN SHRUB ROSES

Variable, versatile and so beautiful

Modern shrub roses have been bred since the turn of the 19th century, and their breeding has become increasingly wide ranging between the wild roses and hybrid kinds as the 20th century has passed. Breeders have introduced roses with specific characteristics that make them almost perfect for solving many garden design problems. From their wild ancestors they get disease resistance and a variety of very useful shapes and sizes – everything from groundcovers to big shrubs. From the old-fashioned roses they have acquired beautiful flower forms and exquisite fragrances. From both sides of their breeding they have received the trait of great hardiness and the ability to adapt and survive in a wide variety of climates.

From the various kinds of large-flowered bush roses, modern shrub roses have inherited long-flowering seasons that may be continuous or occur in repeated cycles of growth and bloom. And many will give an added season of colour with their large and showy hips.

If you want plants with low maintenance and low water needs, modern shrub roses offer unrivalled flower power with fragrances to match on plants that are so hardy and vigorous that they can often be grown where other fine flowering shrubs would fail.

A tall, sprawling shrub, 'Constance Spry', does best when supported on a tripod, small tree or by other shrubs. It has only one heavy flowering season, but the lavish clear pink blooms make it well worth the wait.

WHAT'S IN A (TRADE) NAME?

To protect their investment of years of patience and considerable expense, most rose breeders now register their new creations before they are introduced commercially. Registered roses have a "proper" registered trade name which looks like this: AUSbred. The trade name is usually followed with the date the plant was registered, but this is not always shown. This trade name is known world-wide and is the name by which the owner of the rose variety will license commercial wholesalers around the world.

Each wholesaler has to pay a royalty to the owner of each bush of the registered plant that he/she grows for sale to nurseries and garden centres. The wholesaler can use whatever popular commercial name desired when the plants are tagged for distribution and sale to the public. Thus AUSbred 1984 becomes 'Bredon' at the point of sale.

Often the first three letters of the registered name indicate the name of the owner of the rose variety, e.g., AUS stands for David Austin, LET for Kleine Lettunich, LEN for Louis Lens, POU for the Poulsen nursery, KOR for the Kordes nursery, MEI for the Meilland family. It is possible for the same rose, with one registered name, to have several commercial names; these synonyms are listed in brackets in the text.

Big Shrub Roses

Major features in the garden

Rose plants in this category are so large that in small gardens they could be used as moderate climbers. Grown as shrubs they fill a big area, as much as a small shrubby tree, and with selective pruning they can actually be trained into small, shady trees. Grown this way, they are ideal for planting alongside gateways, or at the corners of buildings where their height keeps the thorns out of the way and their branch patterns, foliage and flowers can be thrown into silhouette against walls or the sky.

Simple needs

Growing is easy; deep, friable, fertile soil, good drainage, an open sunny position and room to spread are the basic requirements. Apply a mulch of straw, stable litter and compost every year, and occasionally bless the plants with blood and bone; water deeply, weekly when the weather gets very hot and drought threatens.

Pruning is simple, too. Form a tree framework – from three to five major trunks, cleared of side shoots, to a height of 2m (6ft) or more. Every year new shoots will burst upward from the base of the plant; retain two or three and remove the rest. Completely cut out a few of the oldest branches each year so that over three or four years all the big branches are renewed by vigorous new growth.

Support the tallest

If grown as climbers, the trunks and branches must be tied firmly against a wall or building to keep them in position. It pays to be very particular about this, as few things are more disappointing than a potentially gorgeous display of flowers completely destroyed by branches flailing around in the wind.

If large shrub roses are set among other shrubs, they will get adequate support from the bushes around them. But when they're used in more open settings, they may need the support of a tripod. Make one from hardwood branches, stripped of their side twigs, from long garden stakes or stout bamboo canes. Alternatively, you can buy metal or wooden supports at many garden centres.

Rodney Hyett (above) / Leigh Clapp (right)

Glorious 'Graham Thomas' (left) makes an impressive display with its yellow blooms against pale green foliage; a sturdy upright grower. The rich pink flowers of 'Gertrude Jekyll' (above) immediately appeal but its thorny growth dictates that it be used away from walkways; a good background shrub.

PLANT VARIETY RIGHTS

Many new rose varieties are protected by plant patents or plant variety rights. It is illegal to propagate these plants for sale without a license from the owner of the plant variety. Strictly speaking, it is illegal to grow cuttings of these roses for private use in your own garden.

'Bloomfield Abundance'

EASY CARE

Tips for success

■ *Planting is easy; deep, friable, fertile soil, good drainage, an open sunny position and room to spread are the basic requirements.*

■ *Apply a mulch of straw, stable litter and compost every year.*

■ *Occasionally bless plants with blood and bone.*

■ *Water deeply and weekly when the weather gets very hot and drought threatens.*

■ *Pruning is simple too. Form a tree framework from three to five major trunks cleared of side shoots to a height of 2m (6ft) or more.*

■ *Every year new shoots will burst upward from the base of the plant; retain two or three and remove the rest.*

■ *Completely cut out a few of the oldest branches each year so that over three or four years all the big branches are renewed by vigorous new growth.*

BIG SHRUB ROSES

Our top choices

- **'Aptos'** (*LET apt*) *1993* – *creamy white semi-double flowers with golden centres are massed over the arching bush in three or more flushes of prolific bloom. At least 2m x 2m (6 x 6ft) but more where conditions are good.*

- **'Beauty of Glenhurst'** *1982* – *a very tall, bushy plant with masses of single pink flowers in huge heads of blossom. The flowers vary from pale to deep pink as they open. The bushes bloom continuously in warm areas, and year-round where there are no winter chills to halt growth or damage the 3m x 3m (10 x 10ft) growth. Sweet perfume.*

- **'Bloomfield Abundance'** *1920* – *often mistaken for 'Cecile Brunner'; the flowers are superficially similar but the bush is much larger and more vigorous, and the flowers are often carried in very large pyramidal heads of buds and blooms. Continuous flowering in warm areas.*

- **'Constance Spry'** *1961* – *a very tall and open shrub which does best when given the support of other shrubs, a small tree or a garden tripod. Large luminous clear pink flowers, cupped and semi-double and with a strong spicy perfume. One heavy flowering season. Easily 3m x 3m (10 x 10ft) in warm areas.*

- **'Doctor Jackson'** (*AUSdoctor*) *1987* – *a vigorous, upright shrub with one heavy display of large scarlet-crimson single blooms carried in big heads of flowers. Large pear-shaped hips follow in autumn and these turn a rich orange as the season progresses. Tall growth with deep green foliage.*

- **'Francis E. Lester'** *1946* – *very strong, vigorous growth that makes an arching open shrub, though it is most often grown as a climber. Masses of pale pink to white single flowers with a strong orange-blossom perfume. Blooms once per season. Growth to at least 3.5m (12ft) tall and as much as 5m (16ft) across the crown.*

- **'Gertrude Jekyll'** (*AUSbord*) *1987* – *tall, vigorous growth that produces medium-sized rich pink, fully-double blooms with old-fashioned muddled centres. Very strong rose fragrance. Very thorny growth so better deployed as a background shrub rather than as a specimen near paths or lawns. Growth to 3m (10ft) tall and somewhat less in width.*

- **'Lichtkonegin Lucia'** (*KORlilub*) *1985* – *clear yellow blooms that retain their colour in the semi-single flowers with three rows of ruffled petals and a centre of golden stamens. Glossy green foliage and growth that reaches about 3m (10ft).*

- **'Graham Thomas'** (*AUSmas*) *1973* – *an eye-stopper of a rose when trained as a climber, or with its supple canes trained to some support. Glorious double, cupped flowers of rich yellow with a strong tea rose perfume. Pale green foliage and some repeat bloom. Revels in warm climates.*

- **'Master Hugh'** *1970* – *a extremely large, open shrub or climber with single, rich rose-pink flowers that are followed by massive bottle-shaped fruits – perhaps the largest of all rose hips. The leaflets are large and set with 9 or 11 on a stalk so the foliage is impressive too. Growth to at least 5m (16ft) tall.*

- **'Mateo's Silk Butterflies'** (*LETsat*) *1992* – *a gorgeous mass of rich pink single flowers with the extra bonus of good drought tolerance and a bush that is continuously in bloom. Growth to 2m (6ft) tall and still growing. Evergreen in warm zones like southern California and Australia.*

- **'Scarlet Fire'** (*same as 'Scharlachglut'*) *1952* – *tall open growth that arches gracefully at about 3m (10ft) to spread 2m (6ft) across in the crown. Abundant, large crimson single flowers with golden stamens and a great crop of big red hips in autumn. An oldie but still one of the best.*

- **'William Baffin'** *1983* – *a tall, arching shrub that is also vigorous and cold tolerant. The shrub repeatedly produces masses of loosely semi-double, open blooms of strawberry-pink softening at the edges to paler pink. Abundant glossy foliage and growth to at least 4m (13ft), lessened by summer pruning after the main crop of flowers.*

- **'Will Scarlet'** *1948* – *a soft shade of scarlet-crimson, the semi-double flowers are carried in small clusters. Growth is upright, well covered in rich green, glossy leaves. Recurrent blooms throughout summer and a happy crop of round red hips in autumn.*

Garry Aitchison

Medium Shrub Roses

Eye-level interest

Medium-sized shrub roses are well suited to suburban and small gardens where unfussy flowering shrubs are required. They can be grouped to create a sense of enclosure and seclusion from the street, or used to add interest to plantings of mixed shrubs. They can look terrific against the sunny side of the house where the perfume will waft in through open doors and windows.

Repeat-flowering varieties will give colour over a long period, but for maximum flowers be sure to regularly remove spent blooms and periodically pinch – prune new growth to induce bushiness.

For example, the several varieties of old-gold, soft apricot and buff-coloured roses included in the following list could be used together with day-lilies, annual flowers, lilies, daisies, yarrows, Gazanias, and silvery leaved plants, such as lamb's ears, snow-in-summer and Artemis. This would create a colour scheme in cream through to soft orange shades, set off by the silvery foliage. It could also include contrasting blues and lavenders, if you like. For more impact, add highlights of scarlet and burnt orange.

Medium shrub roses look solid and tend to anchor designs to the ground. At eye-level, they can create a sense of stability that offers pleasing contrasts with the lighter qualities of climbing and large shrub roses.

Although initially twiggy, 'Mary Rose' mounds up into a fine shrub with large blooms.

Hips an Autumn Bonus

As the flowering season draws to a close, leave the spent flowers in place so that the colourful fruits or hips can develop. Hips are a delightful bonus that mark the end of the flowering year. Left on the bush, they glow in the light of an Indian summer and attract fruit-eating birds to the garden. When ripe and colourful, they can also be used in indoor arrangements.

Mixed Plantings

Medium-sized shrub roses are lovely when used in plantings of mixed shrubs and flowers.

Go for a Good Balance

It is best not to go overboard with too many shrub roses, or with any other kind; the more of one plant family you have in the garden, the more likely that unlovely pests and diseases will proliferate. Mixing shrub roses with other shrubs and flowers will give you many opportunities for creative garden making, whereas collecting only roses may well become an exercise in fitting in "just one more".

In selecting my favourite varieties I have included the very fashionable as well as less well-promoted varieties. They all have fine qualities additional to lovely flowers.

Rodney Hyett (above) / Leigh Clapp (right)

Pretty pink clusters decorate the dark foliage of 'Cornelia'; a good specimen to train as a small climber.

With its 'pompoms' of large apricot flowers, 'Buff Beauty' (above) is a favourite in cottage gardens. Also hard to overlook are the silvery- pink flowers of fragrant 'Felicia' (right); it looks especially appealing cascading over a weathered, grey wooden fence.

MEDIUM SHRUB ROSES

Our top choices

■ **'Andenken an Alma de l'Aigle'**
*1955 – a delightful pale
pink-apricot colour on
semi-double flowers that come
in small clusters. The flowers
are modern-looking and large;
when fully opened they are
deep-centred and invite you to
inhale their fragrance. Bushy
growth to 1.5m (5ft) and a
good crop of bright red fruits.*

■ **'Angela'** *1983 – two rows of
bright pink petals make each
flower light and breezy in
appearance, while great
clusters of bloom cover each
plant in colour. The intensity
of colour is lightened by a white
eye at the centre of each flower.
About 2m (6ft) tall and a little
wider in spread.*

■ **'Belinda's Dream'** *1988 –
large modern flowers of soft pink with a strong perfume
and pleasing blue-green leaves on a shrub about 1.5m
(5ft) or so in all dimensions. Repeat bloom over a long
season. Bred in Texas and so should be really hardy
and adaptable.*

■ **'Birdie Blye'** *1904 – long, pointed buds like those of a
modern rose that open to show off cupped and loosely
double blooms of pale pink. Large clusters mean the
display goes on and on, while repeat bloom gives an*

*The delightful
single flowers of
'Dapple Dawn'
(above) are
borne in large
clusters so that
the bush appears
to be continuously
in flower.*

Don Brice (left) / Paddy Wales (inset) / Rodney Hyett (above)

*overall long season of flowers. Light fragrance, light green
foliage and very cold-hardy growth to at least 1.5m (5ft).
Few thorns are a plus for tender-skinned folk.*

■ **'Blue Boy'** *1958 – a rarely seen treasure, this rose has
large flowers in small clusters; fully double, richly
perfumed and sumptuously coloured in shades of
wine-red, beetroot, purple and everything in between.
Truly distinctive dark, dull foliage dusted silver-blue.
Bushy growth to 2m (6ft), maybe more in mild climates
and lush conditions. Very few thorns.*

■ **'Bonn'** *1950 – a bright scarlet rose with moderate-sized
flowers carried in small nodding clusters. Tall, bushy
growth and bright green glossy foliage. A very cheerful
colour that sparkles among other reds. Achieves 2m (6ft)
in height.*

■ **'Bredon'** *(AUSbred) 1984 – short, compact growth and
continuous bloom make this a valuable garden rose; the
more so because of its soft apricot-buff coloured flowers,
old-fashioned form and rich fruity fragrance.*

■ **'Brother Cadfael'** *(AUSglobe) 1990 – very tall growth,
over 2m (6ft) and deep green foliage that shows off the
large, globular, peony-pink flowers very handsomely.
Repeat blooms throughout summer.*

■ **'Bubble Bath'** *1980 – a large, cascading shrub well
clothed with leaves and masses of soft pink flowers in
good-sized clusters that appear throughout summer. Gentle
rose fragrance. Growth to 3m (10ft) or so.*

The enormous trusses of 'Lavender Lassie' (right) are held aloft by strong canes. This rose takes clipping well and can be used as a climber or a hedge.

- **'Buff Beauty'** *1939 – one of the roses much promoted in the cottage garden revival of the late 80s. Vigorous growth that arches and spreads, inviting treatment as a low climber. Clusters of small apricot and old gold double flowers appear at the ends of the new growth but these fade to almost white in hot climates. Autumn flowers can be especially lovely. In my view, rather too large to be treated as a standard rose but many people choose to use it in this way.*

- **'Cardinal Hume'** *(HARregale) 1984 – a good companion for 'Blue Boy' and other dark red roses, especially when accompanied by masses of silver foliage or plants with greenish-yellow flowers such as Euphorbias, bronze fennel and rue. Spreading growth to about 2m (6ft), more compact in cool areas. Purplish flowers on and off all summer.*

- **'Cornelia'** *1925 – low, spreading growth spangled with coral pink buds and slightly paler semi-double flowers set against dense dark foliage. It can easily be trained as a small climber along a fence. Approximately 2m (6ft) tall and the same in spread.*

- **'Dapple Dawn'** *1983 – an English rose introduced by David Austin has delightful single flowers of warm-pink shades which are borne in large clusters so that the bushes seem to be continuously in flower. Fragrance is excellent, too. Growth to 2m x 2m. One of the best modern shrub roses.*

- **'Dentelle de Malines'** *(LENspink) 1983 – grows tall and wide and is well suited to a small garden. The masses of small baby-pink flowers appear only once but the show is great for three to four weeks. Fair perfume. Grows about 1.5m (5ft) all round.*

- **'Devon'** *(POUlspan) 1993 – delightful semi-double, open flowers in shades of soft lemon with a touch of pale apricot towards the centre on a bush of dense, rich green foliage. Repeated flowering on mounding growth to about 1.5m (5ft) in all directions.*

- **'Felicia'** *1928 – is noted for its strong fragrance as much as its lovely rich silvery pink flowers, which are not easily overlooked. Growth is strong and bushy and the glossy mid-green foliage gives good coverage. Can be grown as a small climber too. Wonderful on old grey wooden fences.*

- **'Golden Wings'** *1956 – has huge single flowers of soft yellow paling a little towards the edges in hot weather. These contrast well with handsome red-brown stamens at the centre of each bloom. Light green leaves on a fairly compact plant that can get as tall as 2m (6ft).*

- **'James Mason'** *1982 – large double flowers of deep crimson-red, double and showing some golden stamens at the centre, are produced in one heavy blooming season. This shrub is vigorous and well branched.*

- **'Jeannie Lajoie'** *1975 – makes strong and vigorous growth to about 2m (6ft) high. It is continuously in bloom, smothered with hundreds of small marshmallow-pink flowers. Very cold tolerant.*

- **'Irene of Denmark'** *1948 – a wonderful shrub rose with dark green foliage and a continuous display of white flowers that have just a hint of cream. Fairly compact, solid growth to about 1.5m (5ft) or sometimes a little taller.*

- **'Lavender Lassie'** *1960 – produces enormous trusses of pink-toned semi-double flowers with hints of lilac. They have a strong fragrance and are set off by dense foliage and held aloft on strong canes. It takes clipping well and can be used as a hedge, or can be tied up as a climber. Mixed with other shrubs, it is superb. Growth to around 4m (13ft).*

- **'Lemon Blush'** *(SIElemon) 1988 – pastel yellow to creamy white blooms that have a soft textured appearance. One heavy show of flowers that have exceptionally rich fragrance. Strong growth to 2m (6ft) high and wide. Very cold hardy.*

- **'Lucetta'** *(AUSemi) 1983 – very feminine semi-double flowers of soft blush-pink that become almost white. The fragrant blossoms are large with big gold stamens and usually come in small clusters on a spreading shrub that can grow about 2m (6ft) across and as much high.*

Rodney Hyett (above) / Don Brice (right)

Continuously in bloom, 'Jeannie Lajoie' has small marshmallow-pink flowers.

Rodney Hyett

The weeping habit of 'Renae' (left) makes it an especially good cottage garden climber while 'Penelope' (above) is useful as a flowering informal hedge.

■ **'Mary Rose' (AUSmary) 1983** – *grows as a compact, twiggy shrub that mounds up into a fine shrub about 2m (6ft) in all directions. The blooms are large, cupped and packed with petals; the fragrance is exceptional and the floral show goes on and on all through summer.*

■ **'Norfolk' (POUfolk) 1989** – *striking spicy pink single flowers with a touch of gold at the centre of each bloom. Continuous bloom on a bush that reaches about 1.5m (5ft) high. Other colours can be found in the group of roses named after English counties.*

■ **'Penelope' 1924** – *produces very large trusses of pale creamy yellow to pale-pink semi-double blooms that have a strong fragrance. Vigorous growth to 2m (6ft) by 1.5 (5ft) makes it useful for a flowering informal hedge, or in a mixed planting or perennials with similar colours.*

■ **'Queen Margethe' (POUlskul) 1994** – *a strong contender for 'Most Beautiful Rose' title. Absolutely delightful fresh pink blooms of old-fashioned style with a wonderful apple-scented perfume and compact growth well clothed in glossy green leaves. Always in bloom. Grows to about 1m (3ft) or a little more.*

■ **'Renae' 1954** – *blooms repeatedly with semi-double pale pink flowers that open wide to reveal a central boss of golden stamens. Sometimes grafted as a standard that grows with a weeping habit but equally as good as a cottage garden climber. Very fragrant.*

■ **'Rochester Cathedral' (HARroffen) 1987** – *richly fragrant double blooms with old-fashioned form and colour; an unusual rose-pink touched with violet. Blooming is repeated several times in one season. Compact growth to about 1.5m (5ft) or more.*

■ **'Rush' (LENmobri) 1985** – *one of the new wild roses with complex breeding that has produced a fine spreading shrub with glossy foliage and arching growth to around 2m (6ft). Clusters of moderate- sized single pink flowers with a white eye repeatedly bloom. The flowers have a delightful fruity perfume.*

■ **'Shady Lady' (MEIsecaso) 1987** – *one of a new race of shade-tolerant roses that are being bred. A long season of semi-double rose-pink flowers paling to white at the centre on a compact bush with plenty of glossy foliage – and it will grow in some shade better than most roses and still flower well.*

■ **'Sharifa Asma' (AUSreef) 1987** – *a sumptuous shallow cup of blush-pink set against mid-green leaves on a compact bush. Very fragrant.*

■ **'Snow Gosling' (POUlgren) 1992** – *a profuse show of double, pure white blooms with a fine fruit fragrance. Growth is compact, bushy and densely covered with solid green leaves. Established plants should be about 1.5m (3ft) tall and as much across.*

SMALL SHRUB ROSES
Perfect for pots

Small shrub roses have some special features which are very useful to garden makers, particularly those with pocket-handkerchief gardens. There are many people too, who have come to gardening later in life and want to enjoy it without it taking over all their leisure time. For these people, small shrub roses are the answer: compact growth, very healthy constitutions, prolific flowering over a long season, many colours and some with excellent fragrances. These roses are well suited to pots and, even if you have enough space for bigger rose plants, you will find that potted roses offer many opportunities to create spots of colour where permanent plantings may not thrive.

You can move potted roses about the garden or patio to create different colour schemes and pleasing associations with other plants as the season passes. For special places, such as beside doors and gates, potted roses give the kind of warm welcome we'd all love to receive.

Of course, small shrub roses can be grown in the garden, too; you'll find that their size makes them ideal for edging garden beds or for underplanting the sunny side of trees or taller shrubs.

SMALL SHRUB ROSES

Pick of the bunch

■ **'Angela Rippon'** *(ocaRU) 1978 – superb rich coral-pink flowers on a compact, dense bush that grows about 75cm (30in) tall. Always a mass of bloom and with a good perfume.*

■ **'Cider Cup'** *(DICladida) 1988 – deep apricot flowers that are fully double and borne in profusion on a compact, bushy plant. It will grow just under 1m (3ft) tall. Continuous bloom set off by mid-green leaves.*

■ **'Glad Tidings'** *(TANtide) 1989 – a glorious dark red rose ideal for small gardens and pot culture. Large clusters of velvet-textured blooms are borne continuously over a long season; dense dark green foliage makes a great foil for the flowers. Growth to about 75cm (30in).*

■ **'Gold Symphonie'** *1994 – described by some as a large-flowered miniature rose, the golden-yellow flowers will be popular in small gardens, however it may be classified. Compact growth to 60cm (2ft).*

■ **'Hakuun'** *1962 – very bushy growth, about 60cm (2ft) tall, covered with small buff-apricot coloured flowers. These fade to almost white with an old gold centre as the flower ages. A prolifically flowering cream rose with good dark foliage and neat growth.*

■ **'New Fashion'** *– loosely semi-double flowers are carried in open clusters that show colours from soft apricot to orange with a golden central cluster of stamens. Ideal companion for soft blue and pale lilac-flowered pot plants, such as Campanulas and Petunias. Grows about 60cm (2ft) high.*

■ **'Morey's Pink'** *1994 – continuous, prolific blooms; a great performer in spots where reliable colour is wanted from late spring until late autumn. The flowers are a soft pink, cupped and semi-double.*

■ **'Sequoia Jewel'** *(MORsewel) 1989 – double, rather globular blooms of glowing cherry-red are freely produced in clusters of about 9 to 15 flowers. Healthy foliage with growth to about 60cm (2ft) high.*

■ **'Sweet Dream'** *(FRYminicot) 1988 – smothered with mouth-watering apricot-peach double blooms. The perfect colour for a Mediterranean-style garden where hues of terracotta and green predominate. Teamed with lavenders, sages and lavender cotton, it imparts a certain amount of class to a garden.*

■ **'Tip Top'** *(TANopel) 1963 – very appealing salmon-pink flowers that are semi-double and open almost flat. Lustrous dark green foliage and compact growth to about 60cm (2ft).*

Garden Picture Library

Ideal for small gardens and pot cultures, 'Glad Tidings' (right) and 'Tip Top' (inset) offer many opportunities to create spots of glorious colour.

OLD-FASHIONED ROSES

Something old, something new

With roses, the term "old-fashioned" doesn't necessarily mean that the variety has been around for a long time. True, some have been grown for centuries but, as newly released roses can also be "old-fashioned", clearly it's not the date of introduction that determines whether or not a rose is so described.

What does determine it is the form of the flower. In old-fashioned roses, the flowers are not high-pointed at the centre like the today's typical rose and the petals do not unfurl in a regular pattern around a central point.

Instead, the centres of old-fashioned roses tend to be low and rounded or even flat across the top surface (e.g., 'Mlle de Sombreuil', inset) and the centres are muddled or quartered (e.g., 'Mme Isaac Pereire' on page 88), some even having a small, green pointel or steeple at the heart of each flower, such as the pictured 'Mme Hardy'.

The most perfect form of old-fashioned rose is the cupped and quartered form, such as is found in 'Koenigin von Danemark'. Roses with this form were developed to the pinnacle of perfection by Dutch and French growers in the late 17th and 18th centuries. Cupped and quartered roses have several rows of outer petals enfolding the quartered heart petals in a cup formation.

Old-fashioned roses were developed by monastic gardeners and apothecaries during the middle ages. In their gardens they grew wild roses for medicinal purposes and gathered together unusual forms of these, such as those with double flowers. With all these "improved" strains clustered together and plenty of bees to cross-pollinate them, even more remarkable roses were sometimes produced from seed.

Among the earliest were the Moss roses, which have buds and stems covered with pine-scented, mossy growths and kinds with striped or spotted flowers. Most of these had quartered, fully double flowers that appeared in one big flush in early summer.

In gardens, old-fashioned roses are hardy and produce masses of sweetly scented flowers on big, spreading shrubs or great thickets. They were favoured by people such as Empress Josephine de Beauharnais, wife of Napoleon, and were used in the romantic English flower gardens of Gertude Jekyll and Vita Sackville-West.

But in today's small gardens, where flowering performance and plant size are important considerations, the modern old-fashioned roses are often better choices. These plants, developed by breeders such as David Austin, John Clements, Andre Eve, Louis Lens, Ralph Moore and others, produce highly fragrant flowers in the old-fashioned form but on much more compact and easily accommodated bushes.

Considered to be one of the most beautifully formed old roses, 'Mme Hardy', (left) features pure white blooms around a small green eye. Inset: 'Mlle de Sombreuil'.

Rodney Hyett

GROUNDCOVER ROSES

Long-flowering, disease-resistant

Prostrate or groundcovering roses are tough, disease resistant and vigorous so they need minimum maintenance. They are also top performers, with loads of flowers smothering the plants from the beginning of the warm weather until the last days of summer, and later still in areas where autumns are mild. Colours range from pure white through cream and many shades of apricot and pink to glowing scarlets and rich wine-reds.

Endless Uses

Imagine sheets of cascading scarlet against the weathered grey surface of a wooden retaining wall, or masses of pale pink tumbling over dark, mossy rocks – wonderful! Some groundcover roses can also be grown in pots and hanging baskets to decorate outdoor living areas, while others look splendid when grown as standards planted in four-square formality. As an added bonus most can be propagated easily from cuttings. However, you cannot sell them as, strictly speaking, it is illegal to grow cuttings of roses protected by plant patents or plant variety rights.

The dimensions that groundcover roses achieve at maturity, say four to five years after they are planted, can vary widely from variety to variety. To achieve a solid mat of weed-free cover, these low-growing roses are usually planted fairly closely together (as per directions on the label). Always plant into soil that has been dug over and enriched with rotted organic matter and a ration of complete plant food, and be very sure that all weeds have been eliminated.

DIMENSIONS

The dimensions given are approximate and based on the plants receiving a "rough" pruning by hedge clippers or brush-cutters each year. Left alone, they will grow thicker and wider.

Disease Resistance

These roses are claimed to be highly disease resistant, so spraying should be unnecessary. But remember, they aren't meant to be inspected as closely as large-flowered bush roses – so don't expect them to be one hundred per cent perfect, just largely trouble free.

If you live in a rainy, humid area, black spot and mildew may still appear, but the plants are said to be vigorous enough to be able to outgrow these troubles. Should a plant develop unacceptable cases of rust, black spot or mildew, throw it away and plant something else. In late winter, trim all over with shears or a brush-cutter.

Leigh Clapp

*A*n old one and still a good one, 'Raubritter' is a modest wiry plant which produces one good display of pink, shell-shaped flowers in early summer. A charming rose which can also be grown as a standard.

GROUNDCOVER COLOUR

Pick of the bunch

With dozens of new cultivars being promoted every year, the choice of groundcover roses is large, and growing larger. Some colourful, vigorous and versatile choices are:

■ **'Coral Meidiland' *(MEIpopul) 1992*** *– a good looking combination of single, coral-pink flowers and bronze-green leaves. Looks great interplanted with silver* **Artemisia** *'Valerie Finnis', or try it with hardy blue bulbs underneath to show off the new bronze leaves in spring.*

■ **'Flower Carpet' *(NOAtraum) 1989*** *– one of the leaders among new multi-purpose roses. Flower Carpet finds landscape use as a groundcover rose with disease-resistant, glossy green foliage and clusters of semi-double blooms of rich, warm pink shades that, with appropriate trimming and pruning, do double duty as a low hedge or border shrub. Small, hard-trimmed plants are suitable as colour spots in hanging baskets and tubs. Growth to about 1.5m (5ft) all round, larger if left unpruned. Also called 'Blooming Carpet' and 'Emera' in some countries.*

■ **'Francine Austin' *TM 1988*** *– one of David Austin's English Roses and very fashionable. Masses of tiny white globular flowers over a long season. Light green foliage. Try it with self-sowing blue Forget-me-nots.*

■ **'Grouse' *(KORimo) 1984*** *– pale pink single flowers with good perfume and solid leaf cover; it looks great tumbling over a wall. At least 3m (10ft) wide and 60cm (2ft) high.*

■ **'Happenstance'** *– a miniature sport of the gigantic 'Mermaid' with pale creamy yellow single flowers and glossy dark green leaves (and plenty of thorns). Growth to about 2 x 2m (6 x 6ft).*

■ **'Kent' *(POUlcov) 1987*** *– open creamy white flowers with two or three rows of petals that set off a golden centre. Bushy spreading growth about 1m (3ft) square.*

■ **'Northamptonshire' *(MATdor) 1990*** *– has very prostrate growth, fragrance and delightful pink and white blooms reminiscent of the Sweetheart Rose ('Cecile Brunner'). Spreads over 1.5m (5ft) and grows about 60cm (2ft) tall.*

■ **'Nozomi' *1968*** *– one of the earliest, low spreading roses to be called a groundcover rose rather than a miniature climber. Arching canes covered with masses of single pale pink and white blooms over one long season. Looks great grown in a large terracotta pot. 2m (6ft) wide by 60cm (2ft) tall.*

Joy Harland (inset above) / Rodney Hyett

84

One of the earliest, low spreading roses to be called a groundcover, 'Nozomi' (left) produces masses of pale pink and white blooms over one long season. 'Flower Carpet' (below) is an excellent pot specimen while 'Suffolk' (inset left) is compact with frequent bursts of bloom.

- **'Partridge'** *1984 – clustered pale pink and white flowers with a single layer of petals sparkle among dark green glossy foliage all summer. 4m (13ft) wide (and more) by 75cm (30in) tall.*

- **'Pearl Meidiland'** *(MEIplatin) 1987 – is very free flowering and has pearl-pink semi-double flowers set against dense foliage. Compact growth suggests planting 1m (3ft) or so apart to get good groundcover.*

- **'Pheasant'** *(KORdapt) 1986 – very deep pink single flowers with a strong perfume appear prolifically on the vigorous growth that will spread about 3m (10ft) and pile up about 75cm (30in) high.*

- **'Raubritter'** *1936 – is a modest wiry plant with refined foliage of neat grey-green and slender growth to about 1m (3ft). It has one good display of perfect shell-shaped, cupped flowers in early summer. A fine warm, pink colour. An old one and a good one.*

- **'Sea Foam'** *1964 – most often seen as a top-heavy standard rose in trendy designer gardens. It is much better grown as a vigorous groundcover where its mounding and cascading dark glossy foliage and flesh-tinted white flowers perform beautifully. A spread of at least 2m (6ft).*

- **'Suffolk'** *(KORmixal) (also called 'Bassino') 1988 – has clear scarlet petals set off by golden stamens at the centre of each single bloom. Compact growth and frequent bursts of bloom. Plant about 1m (3ft) apart for good coverage.*

- **'Temple Bells'** *1971 – produces long, lax canes that stand about 30cm (1ft) above the soil, but spread 3m (10ft). The canes root where they touch the soil, or get buried in mulch so it is a ready grower and great for controlling soil erosion. The masses of white blooms are carried repeatedly. Good in hanging baskets – give the idea a try!*

- **'White Flower Carpet'** *1991 – also known as 'Fragrant White', carries small clusters of creamy-white semi-double flowers continuously as long as water, plant food and sunlight are plentiful. Growth is low and prostrate after trimming, capable of mounding up to 1.5m (5ft) or so. Splendid bank or rockery cover.*

- **'White Meidiland'** *(MEIcoublan) 1987 – lush dark green foliage that is always spangled with clustered small blooms of pure white. Each plant will cover about 1m (3ft) square.*

CLIMBING ROSES

The most romantic roses of all

limbers aren't a separate category of roses because all types of roses have the potential to produce a climbing variety. Some wild roses occur naturally as climbers and some hybrid seedlings develop as climbing forms. Hybrid roses of all kinds can develop an exceptionally tall and vigorous shoot which, when isolated and propagated, can be regarded as a climbing rose.

Beautiful, But ...

Many gardeners consider climbing roses to be the most romantic and useful of all. In full bloom they have few rivals, their masses of often fragrant flowers creating a breathtaking impression.

They're also marvellous screening plants, which can be used to disguise a ramshackle shed, or create a barrier against prying eyes; train a climber along a fence to add height to your garden, or over an archway to create a fragrant, and eventually, shady nook.

But beautiful as they are, there's a downside. You'll find climbing roses are time consuming. There are a small number that require little care, and a number that produce prolific flower displays, making them invaluable in developing the landscape around homes.

One or two might be lovely, but more mean a lot of effort to get them pruned and tied into position. In cold climates they have to be mounded and "winterised" as well – and undone again as spring approaches.

How to Hold Them Up

Roses are not naturally equipped with apparatus for climbing; they don't twist around supports and neither do they have twining tendrils or adhesive pads with which to climb. It is their nature for one stem to scramble over another, or through and over a nearby shrub, and to stay up securely they need to be tied to whatever you want them to grow on.

A trellis of some sort is the usual support, since the long canes can be easily tied to it and just as easily untied. Don't be tempted to twine the rose canes under and around a supporting trellis. This makes endless work when pruning time comes as it all has to be unwound, and since old rose canes are not always pliable, there is the risk of damage.

Tie the rose canes to the outside surface of the framework instead.

Routine Maintenance

Modern large-flowered climbing roses generally need their flowering branches replaced every three to four years. After this time, old branches tend to lose their vigour and produce few flowers. Strong new growth usually appears every year after the first flush of flowers, and several of these branches should be selected each year as replacements for unproductive branches. Cut out the old, unproductive canes completely, then tie the young, new canes into place.

Leigh Clapp / Garden at Red Cow Farm

More than just a pretty face! 'Zéphirine Drouhin' is popular not only because of its long-flowering satiny pink blooms, but also for its strong fragrance and lack of thorns. A great choice for a busy doorway or oft-used path.

COMPACT CLIMBERS

■ **'Alchemist'** *1956* – *a luscious blend of creams and soft coppery gold tones, sometimes tinted with red. Fully double flowers are wonderfully fragrant. Once-blooming but worth the space. Shiny bronze-green foliage.*

■ **'Crested Sweetheart' (MORsweet)** – *an old-fashioned looking rose bred in 1988. A low climber to about 2.5m (8ft), it has heavily crested mossing on the buds, just as old Moss roses have. Flowers are soft pink, fully double and very fragrant.*

■ *Climbing* **'Iceberg'** – *dating from 1968, this climbing version of the universally grown bush rose is just as good as its namesake; perfect where a touch of white is needed in a garden plan.*

■ **'Jacqueline du Pré' (HARwanna)** *1989* – *may be treated as a compact climber or as a shrub rose. Continuous blooms with excellent perfume and growth to about 3m (10ft) tall and as wide. Beautiful pale shell-pink semi-double flowers with conspicuous red stamens – lovely!*

■ **'Madame Ernst Calvat'** *1888* – *pale pink with lilac overtones, fully double-cupped and quartered, well scented with growth to 3m (10ft). A subtle and beautiful reminder of just how well 19th century rose breeders could spot winners.*

■ **'Madame Isaac Pereire'** *1881* – *rich rose-magenta colour, fully double in the old-fashioned form, strong scent with growth to 3m (10ft) and more. One of the best old roses and still one of the most satisfying of all roses.*

■ **'Maigold'** *1953* – *semi-double flowers of rich golden-apricot and yellow, glossy rich green leaves with arching, thorny growth that is best hidden by honeysuckle or some other light climber. One prolific flower season in early summer. Growth to 4m (13ft).*

■ **'Noella Nabonnand'** *1901* – *a soft, magenta-beetroot colour which mixes well with other dark colours in the purple- to wine-red shades, or which goes well with selected pink flowers backed up with silver perennials. Large open semi-double flowers with good perfume on a moderate climber.*

■ **'Paul's Lemon Pillar'** *1915* – *elegant, pale, lemon-yellow flowers on sparse growth to 3m (10ft) and more. Strongly scented but only one season of fabulous bloom.*

■ **'Pierre de Ronsard' (MEIviolin)** – *a newcomer from 1987 that has stayed the distance to become a classic climber with all the best qualities of old and new; delicious pale pink and cream old-fashioned flowers with continuous flowering and good disease resistance. Fair scent.*

■ **'Zéphirine Drouhin'** *1868* – *the absence of thorns is the first attraction for many gardeners, but it's the strongly perfumed, satiny pink flowers that are the main event. They appear prolifically over a long season on a plant that grows to 4m (13ft) and more. There is also a much paler sport called 'Kathleen Harroop', which is also a fine rose.*

Compact climbers include 'Pierre de Ronsard' (right) and 'Madame Isaac Pereire' (below). Climbing 'Pinkie' (far right) is both a compact and easy-care climber.

Leigh Clapp (left) / Rodney Hyett (inset) / Don Brice (above and above right)

EASY-CARE CLIMBERS

If all the maintenance sounds like too much effort, consider the following climbers. They are all suited to small
gardens and need little pruning other than to remove dead
wood. Overgrowth reaching into path space and garden
beds can be cut away anytime; yearly overall pruning will
serve only to limit the display of flowers. Alas, none is
reliably cold tolerant beyond about -5˚C (23˚F).

■ **'Fortune's Double Yellow' (*Rosa* x *odorata*
'Pseudindica')** *1845 – an elegant climber from
ancient China. Cupped, loosely double-apricot yellow
flowers are heavily stained with crimson; its name
belies its appearance – in its time it was the closest to
yellow of any climber. Once-flowering but wonderful
trailing through the branches of an old pear tree, or
any mature deciduous fruit tree with white flowers.
Not cold-tolerant. Almost never needs pruning.*

■ **Rosa laevigata (syn. R. sinica alba)** – *a wild rose
from China that has been grown in European and
American gardens for centuries. Glossy, large, bright
green leaves set off to perfection a massive spring
show of single white flowers. While it can grow to
6m (20ft) and more, it seems not to mind smaller
premises and will take moderate pruning.*

■ **Climbing 'Pinkie'** *1952 – close jointed growth that
makes a compact climber with dense foliage and a prolific
display of semi-double, rich deep pink blooms. Not many
thorns, so perfect for archways and verandah posts.*

■ **Climbing 'Pompon de Paris'** *1839 – small rose-pink
flowers on twiggy growth to about 2.5m (8ft). Flowers
lavishly produced in early summer with a few to
follow later in the season. Very good for small gardens
and tight corners so long as it gets plenty of sun.*

CLIMBERS FOR COTTAGE CHARM

Cottage gardens feature a profusion of romantic, old-fashioned, and highly perfumed flowers, herbs and fruit trees – all together they mean constant work. These climbing roses are suitable for training on verandah posts to create the atmosphere of a cottage garden all by themselves.

■ **'Black Boy'** *1919 – a lustrous, dark wine-red rose, even darker on the underside of each petal, blessed with a pronounced perfume. This rose has exerted a strong sentimental pull on Australian gardeners for at least three generations. Blooms are semi-double, somewhat globular in form, and carried in small clusters. Repeat blooming from early summer until autumn. Sparse foliage that can be best hidden among the foliage of a supporting shrub such as Cotinus coggygria 'Royal Purple' – the Smoke Bush.*

■ **'Crépuscule'** *1904 – one of the all time greats, yet all too rarely seen. Growth is compact, foliage healthy and dense with masses of medium-sized, gold and yellow flowers produced in small clusters. Splendid on its own or glorious growing with soft blue companion plants. The rfume is sweet and far reaching. Not very cold-tolerant, but a great plant for mild climates.*

■ **'Lamarque'** *– a delightful concoction of fully double, old-fashioned, cupped, and quartered flowers in creamy white. Raised in 1830, it has been popular ever since. It is intolerant of cold conditions and does well in mild, warm, dry and subtropical areas. About 5m (16ft) if it is left unpruned, otherwise, with some gentle trimming, a neat, shrubby climber.*

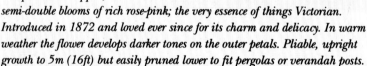
'Crepuscule'   'Titian'

■ **'La Reine Victoria'** *– small but regal flower with real presence. Cupped, semi-double blooms of rich rose-pink; the very essence of things Victorian. Introduced in 1872 and loved ever since for its charm and delicacy. In warm weather the flower develops darker tones on the outer petals. Pliable, upright growth to 5m (16ft) but easily pruned lower to fit pergolas or verandah posts.*

■ **'Mrs F. W. Flight'** *– a cluster-flowered modest climber dating from 1905. It produces one heavy crop of semi-double, soft rose-pink flowers in early summer. Still very popular in France and southern Europe and now reappearing in American lists. Healthy growth to 3.5m (12ft) with plenty of leaf cover to set off the masses of flowers.*

■ **'Paul Transon'** *– an old rose from 1900. Its glorious, soft apricot-pink, double flowers are such charmers and its healthy, glossy green leaves and moderate growth make it valued still. The colour easily fits in with blue or pink schemes. Pliable growth to 4m (13ft).*

■ **'Primevere'** *1929 – the very best medium-small, cluster-flowered yellow climber. Wins hands down from all others. Bright yellow, fully double flowers that develop to rich cream as they mature. The flowers are carried in small clusters and appear over a long season. Well perfumed. Great with all things blue, lavender, cream, yellow and white.*

■ **'Titian'** *– great, blowzy, semi-double blooms of rich cherry-pink on a compact climber. Raised in Australia in 1950 and suited to warm, dry climates where it performs over a long season and produces especially beautiful flowers in autumn. Little known but excellent.*

■ **'Veilchenblau'** *1909 – smoky purple-blue that fades to grey and lavender as the flowers age. Many small, semi-double flowers in compact clusters along the long, pliable canes. Once-blooming and blessed with a strong citrus perfume. No thorns and good, healthy foliage.*

'La Reine Victoria'

Leigh Clapp / Garden at Red Cow Farm (right)

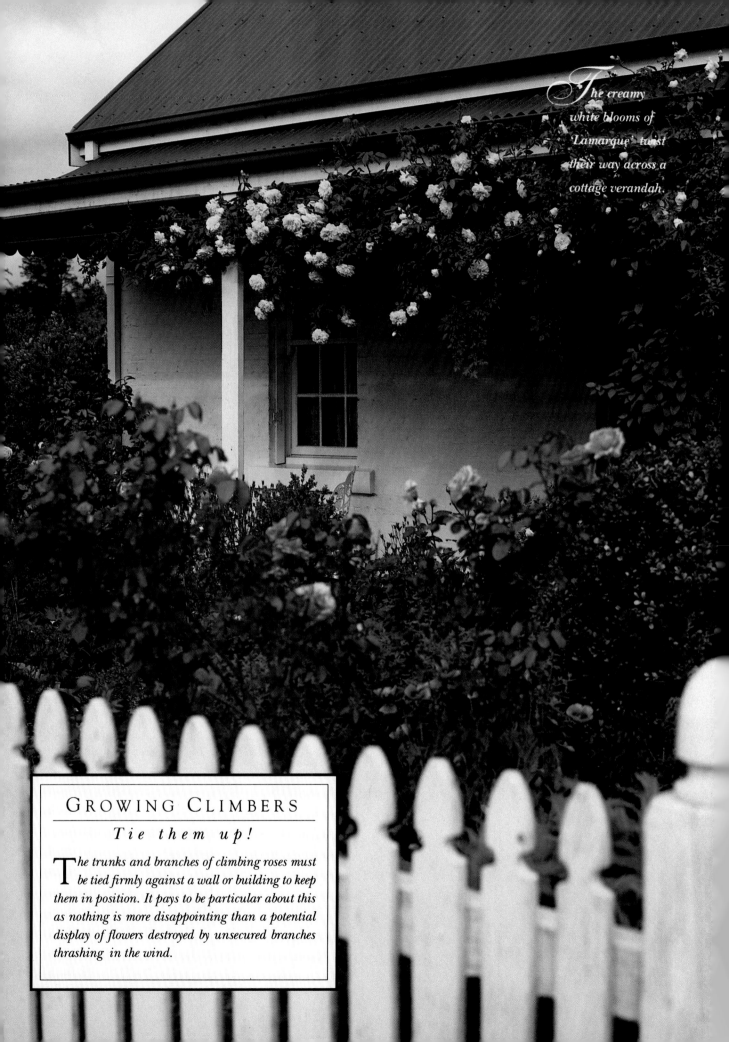

The creamy white blooms of 'Lamarque' twist their way across a cottage verandah.

GROWING CLIMBERS

Tie them up!

The trunks and branches of climbing roses must be tied firmly against a wall or building to keep them in position. It pays to be particular about this as nothing is more disappointing than a potential display of flowers destroyed by unsecured branches thrashing in the wind.

Big, Bold Climbers

Growth of these climbers is strong and vigorous, and all produce a breath-taking show of flowers. To achieve the best possible display of flowers, the long canes and side branches should be pruned by about one-third their length in late autumn or winter, and carefully tied with strong twine to verandah posts and barge boards so they they do not thrash around in the wind. One plant of any of the grand roses listed here gives great returns; two might be more than you have the energy to prune!

- **'Belle Portugaise'** *1903 – large, open, semi-double blooms in pale pink that flourish for an all-too-short season in late spring. A knock-out in its time, and still a great verandah rose today. Will easily attain 4m (13ft) and more in frost-free areas.*

- **'Cerise Bouquet'** *1958 – makes up in flower number what each bloom lacks in size. Tall growth and arching; great for covering an unsightly shed or garage. Small grey-green ferny leaves and abundant, fully double, cerise flowers in one massive early summer show. Growth to 5m (16ft) and more. Does not respond well to pruning, other than the removal of dead wood or wayward branches that threaten to snag passers-by.*

- **'Madame Gregoire Stachelin'** *1927 – very large, open semi-double blooms of soft pink. One heavy flowering season followed by magnificently large orange hips. A fine rose for training on a verandah where it will have no trouble covering 5m (16ft) at least.*

- **'(Mlle de) Sombreuil'** *1850 – very full, double rose of creamy white, well scented and strikingly beautiful in its old-fashioned formation. Growth to 5m (16ft) or so; flowers over a long season. Light pruning is strongly recommended.*

LEFT OUT IN THE COLD

Until recently climbing roses in cold climates have required arduous preparation to adequately insulate them from winter freezing. Happily now there are roses that are tolerant of extreme cold. Here is our selection of the best.

- **'Captain Samuel Holland'** *1990 – can be a spreading shrub but is best treated as a pillar rose and tied to a verandah post. Cheery, double and a strong shade of red with flowers borne in clusters over a long season. Growth and leaves are disease resistant. Will grow to about 3m (10ft).*

- **'Henry Kelsey'** *1984 – bright red, semi-double blooms that open to show off a mass of golden stamens at the centre of each bloom. By reputation it is extremely cold hardy. The foliage is healthy and glossy. Strong arching growth to about 3m (10ft).*

- **'John Cabot'** *1978 – can be treated as a climber or as a very large shrub rose. The semi-double deep rose-pink flowers are carried in repeated bursts of bloom over a long season on strong, arching growth that is well clothed with leaves. Plants will grow to about 3m (10ft).*

- **'John Davis'** *1986 – has outstanding cupped and quartered flowers of rich pink. Golden stamens show at the centre when the flowers are fully opened by the sun. Strong growth to 3m (10ft) and healthy foliage produce flowers in repeated bursts of bloom.*

- **'William Baffin'** *1983 – a particularly vigorous plant that can reach about 3.5m (12ft) in height. The almost single flowers are an eye-catching strawberry-pink with a white eye at the centre, and a fine display of contrasting gold stamens at the heart.*

SOME LIKE IT HOT

These climbers have been bred from roses that originated in the gardens of southern China. They are intolerant of cold winds and frosty weather, and can be severely debilitated, even killed, by hard frosts; they revel in warm to hot subtropical climates.

- **'Céline Forrestier'** *1858 – pale yellow to creamy white double flowers are borne in small clusters over an extended season. The close jointed growth builds up to make a compact climber, providing pruning is light. Dense light green foliage an excellent foil for flowers. Growth to about 4m (13ft) but as canes are lax they will need support to reach upwards to about 3m (10ft).*

- **'Desprez a' fleur jaune'** *1830 – cupped and quartered soft yellow flowers in small clusters. Compact growth to 3m (10ft) makes it an ideal plant for a small garden or courtyard. In warm protected situations the plant flowers virtually non-stop.*

- **'Madame Alfred Carrière'** *1879 – white with a pink blush, large flowers and tall growth well covered with heavy, deep green foliage. Small clusters of blooms are carried at almost every growing point along the canes so that the flower season is long and prolific. Double flowers and centre petals muddled in snowy white swirls.*

- **'William Allen Richardson'** *1878 – faded apricot-gold petals muddled together in medium to small flowers in clusters of three to five buds. Old flowers and newly opened buds show a colour range from creamy white with a touch of deeper colour at their centres to rich egg yolk-yellow shades. Compact climber to 3m (10ft) that responds well to light pruning.*

Both 'Madame Alfred Carrière' (right) and 'William Allen Richardson' (above) revel in subtropical climates. 'Madame Gregoire Stachelin' (above left) is a big, showy climber.

Rodney Hyett (left) / Don Brice (far left)

ROSES FOR HEDGES

Beautiful and secure

he idea of using roses as hedges is as old as time. Roses are an ideal choice. Their thorns and interlocking branches make them natural barrier plants, and the blooms are a bonus.

But what if you want an open outlook to the view beyond?

There is a group of low, spreading roses that provide the answer. Their thorny interlocking branches make a dense network of stems just above ground level, so that they don't impede the view into the garden, or out of it. Most often such barrier roses are used in places where public access needs to be controlled without resorting to obtrusive or hostile-looking fencing.

These roses are very tough and drought-tolerant, but if they are to perform well as barrier plants they need to be growing vigorously and to be in good health; therefore do ensure that roses planted for this purpose are well fed and watered.

The best pruning technique is to go over them with electric hedge clippers in late winter or very early spring. Plants do not need to be individually pruned. To make them effective as a barrier, plant fairly closely and in a deep enough band to discourage people and animals from trying to cross over. This may sound pretty grim, but bear in mind that the plants, properly cared for, will usually be a mass of bloom – the thorns will be out of sight underneath.

Photos Horticultural / Don Brice (inset)

Rosa 'Ferdy' (left) grows into an effective low hedge, while 'Perle d'Or' (inset) is a little larger and would be suitable to grow along a pathway.

Leigh Clapp (left) / Joy Harland (right)

LOW HEDGES

Pick of the bunch

- **'Borderer'** *1918* – *raised in Australia, this hardy and very floriferous bush is hardly ever without a flower or two, and in the warm months is covered in bloom. Semi-double flowers of warm, peach-pink shades and low, dense twiggy growth that needs clipping only once a year to keep it in shape.*

- **'Nearly Wild'** *1941* – *a very hardy plant which has a profuse show of single pink blooms along its long low canes in late spring. Hundreds upon hundreds of flowers open at a time; a stunning sight. Grows 75cm (30in) high and more than 1m (3ft) across.*

- **'Moonsprite'** *1956* – *a surprising small plant which mounds into a bush about 1m (3ft) tall and as much across, and is covered in dark green leathery foliage. Old-fashioned style flowers are highly fragrant, fully double and pure white. Always in bloom. Planted closely, 1m (3ft) apart, this rose is an ideal thick, low barrier against small animals.*

- **'Pearl Drift'** *(LEGgab) 1981* – *produces sheets of big, semi-double white flowers flushed with pale pink above dark green foliage that mounds and sprawls to about 1m (3ft) high and 1.5m (5ft) across. Continuous blooms. Does well in shade and a very tough plant; an all-round performer.*

- **'Simon Robinson'** *(TRObwich) 1982* – *a compact, spreading plant with masses of bright pink single blooms continuously in flower. Planted about 1m (3ft) apart the plants will mesh together to make a good defence about 75cm (30in) high.*

- **'The Reeve'** *1969* – *the breeder of this plant, David Austin, describes it as a rather floppy shrub; nevertheless that habit is an asset here as the spreading growth of over 1m (3ft) in height has an armature of stout thorns which act as a great deterrent. The double flowers are deep pink and are backed up with small dark foliage.*

Other varieties to consider

- **'Baby Faurax'** – *lilac-mauve*
- **'Ballerina'** – *single, pink with a white eye*
- **'Carefree Wonder'** *(MEIpitac)* – *bold strong pink, shading lighter*
- **'Carabella'** – *single, blush-pink*
- **'China Doll'** – *china-pink*
- **'Ferdy'** *(KEItoly)* – *coral-pink*
- **'La Sevillana'** *(MEIgekanu)* – *scarlet*
- **'Mr Bluebird'** – *purple-blue*
- **'Pinkie', 'Pink La Sevillana'** *(MEIgeroko)* **and 'Simply Magic'** *(MEItobla)* – *clear rose-pink*
- **'Sweet Chariot'** *(MORchari)* – *wine-mulberry purple*
- **'The Fairy'** – *pale pink*

A FLOWERING HEDGE

Keep it simple

Not all roses suitable for hedging will flower at the same time, nor will they necessarily have foliage of a similar size, colour or density. For uniformity of appearance and to ensure simultaneous flowering along the entire edge, use only one type of rose in a hedge.

With their spreading habits, 'The Reeve' (seen at left with 'Penelope') and ' The Fairy' (above) make ideal choices for low hedging.

MEDIUM-SIZED HEDGES

Perfect for driveways

Left alone, these roses will make bushes 2m (6ft) tall and almost as wide; pruned they can be happily contained to much lower and less spreading dimensions. All are repeat-flowering plants that look good lining paths and driveways. Pruned, they also make lovely low to medium-sized hedges.

- **'Bonica' (MEIdomonac) 1985** – *carries very large clusters of semi-double soft pink flowers that are apple scented, a refreshing change to the floral bouquets of most rose perfumes. Growth is compact, vigorous and well clothed with glossy green leaves.*

- **'Cecile Brunner'** – *a well-loved old rose with abundant flowers, sweet perfume and healthy growth. The bushes are well covered with light green foliage tinged with red when newly emerging. The flowers are baby pink in colour. Often called the 'Sweetheart Rose'. First sold in 1881.*

- **'Clotilde Soupert'** – *can create an instant atmosphere of yesterday with its flat-faced, fully double blooms of pale pink. Dating from 1890, its delicate, old-fashioned appearance belies its hardy qualities, proving once again that old roses are stayers and can still be great players.*

- **'Cramoisi Superieur'** – *another old rose that has been grown in gardens since 1832 and is still going strong. Vivid scarlet flowers are carried year round in warm areas and elsewhere over an extended season.*

- **'Lady Ann Kidwell'** – *produces long elegant buds from which unfurl wine-red 'butterfly bows', named for the free and loosely arranged rolled and quilled petals. The flowers are semi-double and gently scented. Introduced in 1948 and found in old Californian gardens.*

- **'Marie Pavie' 1888** – *produces good-sized clusters of small, semi-double blooms which are pale blush-pink fading to almost white in warm weather. A long blooming season.*

- **'Perle d'Or'** – *dating from 1883, this rose closely resembles 'Cecile Brunner' except for the gold colour of its flowers.*

- **'Pink Gate Rose'** – *more open in its flowers than 'Cecile Brunner' and somewhat larger, in warm areas it may grow taller and wider too. A "found" rose from California, its original name has been lost. A fine healthy rose with lovely flowers.*

- **'Sophie's Perpetual'** – *another "found" rose, this time from England. Deep rose-pink semi-double flowers on compact growth.*

- **'White Cecile Brunner'** – *a fine, creamy white version of its well-known namesake. First recorded in 1909.*

Leigh Clapp

The 'Sweetheart Rose' – 'Cecile Brunner' – grows into a sturdy, perfumed hedge adorned with abundant blooms.

PRIVACY HEDGES

These are naturally bushy, tall-growing plants. They need very little attention apart from occasional trimming to encourage dense twiggy growth, and the periodic removal of dead branches. Regular watering and feeding, as for all roses, will produce better growth and more flowers.

■ **'Darlow's Enigma'** – *a sprawling, dense grower for a shrub that eventually gets to about 2m (6ft), or maybe a little larger, with a spread of about 3m (10ft). Wonderfully fragrant with rich, glossy foliage.*

■ **'Sally Holmes'** *1976* – *prolific, ivory-white flowers that are single and elegant on an outstanding, bushy compact plant. Grows into an effective barrier almost 2m (6ft) tall and 1m (3ft) wide. At the base of a downhill excavation, it makes a great stop-all and a lovely scene in a hard-to-landscape area.*

■ **'Westerland'** *1969* – *a hardy, cold-resistant rose with glorious coppery orange flowers and strong, vigorous growth. Free flowering and with plenty of good, glossy foliage. Height over 2m (6ft) and about the same width.*

FRAGRANCE

The rose's great gift to gardens

Some people claim to be able to detect a thousand and one nuances of various scents in one fragrant rose bloom. Such finesse is not very useful to the average gardener with an average sense of smell. Most of us can detect a few basic undertones in the perfume of a rose; those that come readily to mind are floral, spicy, fruity and musky. Sometimes these are individually pronounced, but most often they are there as part of the overall perfume. They all add immensely to the pleasure given by the rose; carried afar on a quiet, late afternoon in autumn, trapped in some still, sunny corner, or only found by actually putting the blossom to your nose, the perfume of a rose is always memorable, romantic and calming to the senses. However, there are some roses that lack scent; this is a result of breeding for roses with particular features in mind, such as colour and flower forms. In the process these improvements are gained at the expense of diminished perfume.

HEAVEN SCENT

While perfumes are most obvious early in the morning or in the cool of early evening, they are always present and can be refreshing at anytime. These roses are not only delightfully fragrant in the garden; their fine perfumes can be preserved in pot-pourri and, of course, the flowers can be cut for inside use. There is much enjoyment to be had in making and giving rose products. Our rose petal oil recipe overpage makes a delightful gift.

Roses mentioned in this book that are strongly or distinctively perfumed are:
'Alchemist', 'Anne Endt', 'Angela Rippon', 'Applejack', 'Belinda's Dream', 'Betty Prior', 'Black Boy', 'Blue Boy', 'Bonica', 'Bredon', 'Chrysler Imperial', 'Constance Spry', 'Corylus', 'Crested Sweetheart', 'Darlow's Enigma', 'Dearest', 'Felicia', 'Fimbriata', 'Fragrant Cloud', 'Francis E. Lester', 'Gertrude Jekyll', 'Graham Thomas', 'Henry Hudson', 'Honeysweet', 'Jens Munk', 'Lavender Lassie', 'Lemon Blush', 'Les Sjulin', 'Louis Jolliet', 'Maid of Honour', 'Mary Rose', 'Mme Isaac Periere', 'Moonsprite', 'Mrs B. R. Cant', 'Mrs John Laing', 'Paul Neyron', 'Paul's Lemon Pillar', 'Primevere', 'Queen Margrethe', Rosa Californica 'Plena', 'Rush', 'Sarah van Fleet', 'Sharifa Asma', 'Snow Gosling', 'Spirit of Peace', 'Zéphirine Drouhin'.

A richly coloured cerise-pink, the blooms of Zéphirine Drouhin are deliciously perfumed, and the stems thornless. A climber, it also garners praise for its long-flowering season.

Leigh Clapp

ROSE PETAL BATH OIL

1 cup fresh rose petals
1½ cups sunflower oil

Pack rose petals into a clean glass jar. Gently warm oil in saucepan over a very low heat. Pour oil over petals; seal jar. Stand jar in a sunny place for 2 weeks, shaking jar each day. Pour oil and petals into saucepan, warm oil slightly in saucepan on very low heat; strain through a double layer of muslin; discard petals. Pour oil into sterilised bottles; seal. *Makes about 1½ cups.*

Leigh Clapp (left)/ Don Brice (inset & right)

Consider the butter yellow of Graham Thomas (inset), the lush wine-red of Black Boy (left), or the small, clear pink clusters of Bonica (below) to add both fragrance and colour to your garden. Bonica has a spreading habit, which enables it to be trained into a particularly attractive standard.

GROWING AND MAINTAINING ROSES

A practical guide to rose care

R oses, despite their delicate beauty, do not require elaborate care. They are remarkably hardy and resilient – just look at the bushes that have survived and thrived in old cemeteries and abandoned homesteads. Some people believe that pruning is a crucial, meticulous task, but as you will find in this chapter, there's no need to fear the shears. In fact, some roses, such as the new, long-flowering groundcovers, are meant to be clipped all over once a year with a chainsaw or brush-cutter. By carrying out just a few basic requirements, and preventative measures to control pests and diseases, you can achieve a delightful display in your garden. It's so easy when you know how!

Leigh Clapp

Raised in Australia in 1950, 'Titian' is well suited to warm, dry climates where it performs over a long season. A compact climber, its rich cherry-red blooms look wonderful tumbling over fences and frames.

Consider the fine fragrance of 'Dainty Bess' (left), the curving canes of 'Canary Bird' (below), or the floriferous 'Safrano' (right) for your garden.

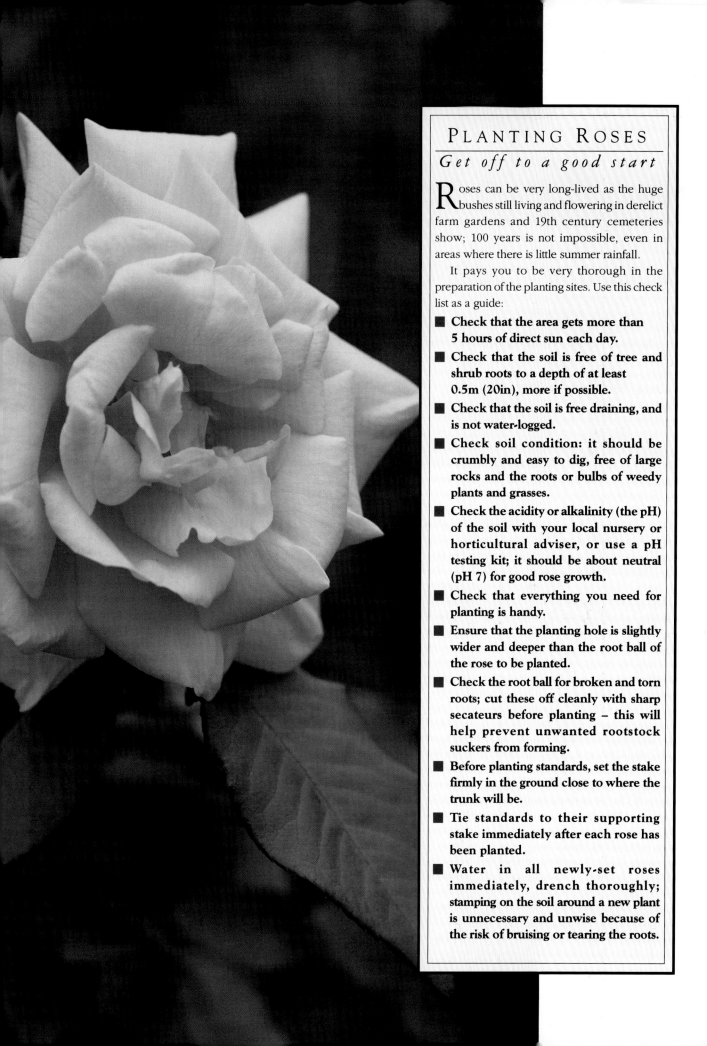

PLANTING ROSES
Get off to a good start

Roses can be very long-lived as the huge bushes still living and flowering in derelict farm gardens and 19th century cemeteries show; 100 years is not impossible, even in areas where there is little summer rainfall.

It pays you to be very thorough in the preparation of the planting sites. Use this check list as a guide:

■ **Check that the area gets more than 5 hours of direct sun each day.**

■ **Check that the soil is free of tree and shrub roots to a depth of at least 0.5m (20in), more if possible.**

■ **Check that the soil is free draining, and is not water-logged.**

■ **Check soil condition: it should be crumbly and easy to dig, free of large rocks and the roots or bulbs of weedy plants and grasses.**

■ **Check the acidity or alkalinity (the pH) of the soil with your local nursery or horticultural adviser, or use a pH testing kit; it should be about neutral (pH 7) for good rose growth.**

■ **Check that everything you need for planting is handy.**

■ **Ensure that the planting hole is slightly wider and deeper than the root ball of the rose to be planted.**

■ **Check the root ball for broken and torn roots; cut these off cleanly with sharp secateurs before planting – this will help prevent unwanted rootstock suckers from forming.**

■ **Before planting standards, set the stake firmly in the ground close to where the trunk will be.**

■ **Tie standards to their supporting stake immediately after each rose has been planted.**

■ **Water in all newly-set roses immediately, drench thoroughly; stamping on the soil around a new plant is unnecessary and unwise because of the risk of bruising or tearing the roots.**

Roses in Pots

Their special needs

As a general rule potted standard roses, or any other kinds of roses grown in pots, need careful watering and feeding. In addition, standards must be tied to a small, strong stake to prevent wind damage.

Roses grown as pot plants in warm, dry climates may need daily watering in hot weather, especially if grown in terracotta pots (which are porous). The use of water-retentive soil additives is another way to overcome water loss in hot weather, but be sure to follow the directions carefully and don't be lulled into not checking the plants and their soil daily. It is possible also to arrange a micro-irrigation system using drippers (not sprays), and as well there are self-watering pots large enough for roses.

To protect potted roses from overheated soil, stand them among other pots so that they partly shade each other; arranging combinations of foliage and flowers this way can be fun as well as practical and can produce lovely effects. Don't be tempted to move potted roses into shaded positions in warm, sunny weather; they won't like it and will not flower at all.

Soils for Potted Roses

"Soils ain't soils" – in fact most potting soils used these days aren't soil at all. They are a blend of rotted pine bark, sand and peat moss (or some similar water-retentive substitute), and as such they do not always satisfy the needs of plants growing in pots for a long time.

Potting Mix + Soil = Body

The 'Iceberg' (left) needs close attention to keep it from drying out in this terracotta pot. Better to position it with other potted plants to give some shade, as the owners have done with the potted plants above.

Many gardeners wanting to grow roses in pots add a shovelful of real garden soil to each bag of bought potting mix and blend it well before planting. This additional soil serves not to feed the plants set in it, but to make the potting mix more substantial. Most people feel it also helps to retain moisture in climates where summer temperatures

Joy Harland (left) / Leigh Clapp

are high. Undoctored potting mixes need watering every day, sometimes twice a day, in very hot weather. Clearly, this is impractical and demands a lot of precious water. Giving the potting soil more body through the addition of some real soil may not be scientifically proven as a means of improving water retention, but it does seem to work.

Water Storing Crystals

Also available are chemical water-retaining gels and crystals that are mixed with potting soils and which serve the same purpose. These need to be renewed periodically before the main growing season – a busy time for many gardeners when the task is all too easily overlooked in favour of more promising work.

Feeding and Mulching Roses

Whether planted in pots or in the garden, all roses need feeding regularly.

To potted roses, fertiliser is best applied in small doses frequently, with each dose being applied to already moist potting mix. An exception to this is slow-release granules – apply these as per the directions on the packet, being sure to scratch the granules lightly into the surface. In the case of plants established in the ground, one generous dressing of complete plant food at the end of winter should suffice. To this must be added a deep and generous quantity of loose mulch, such as stable litter, pea straw, plain wheat straw, spoiled straw, composted sawdust, buzz-saw chips or shredded garden clippings – in fact anything that will serve to keep the soil cool, help to retain water and slowly rot down to add its own goodness to the soil.

It is a good idea to use old newspapers as the first layer of such a garden mulch; they are excellent weed-proof mats and in time will rot down to nothing. Spread whole sections of the daily broadsheet over the soil and weeds. Then cover with whatever organic mulch can be had for the least expense – and that is that. Do not stint; pile it on thickly – 30cm (12in) is not too deep. And do remember that it must be renewed as it settles and rots. A light dusting of blood and bone, "Complete D" or any fertiliser with a high nitrogen content will eliminate any risk of a temporary nitrogen deficiency.

Mulching is an annual task. Such blankets of "goodies" must be renewed at least annually to ensure that they keep weeds down and minimise the upward splash of rain water that could carry diseases from the surface of the soil to the lower leaves of the plants.

How to Prune Roses

It's easy when you know how

What is common to all roses is toughness. You won't kill a rose by pruning it, no matter when or how you do it. You might not get any flowers that year, but that's the worst you can do. Clearly, for maximum bloom, it's best to prune at

Andre Martin (inset) / Leigh Clapp

PRUNER'S TOOLKIT

Make sure all the items are of good quality

1 pair secateurs

1 short pruning saw

1 pair long-handled "lopping" snips

1 pair leather gauntlet gloves

The brilliant red flowers of 'Altissimo' are carried in clusters near the end of canes, making it a superb rose for a trellis or verandah post.

the right time of year and, for appearance sake, to do it with some sensitivity, but in the average garden there's no need to be fearful of pruning.

In many parks and rose gardens, roses are pruned by machine – a petrol driven slasher/mower with blades raised up to about 75cm high on a pair of bicycle wheels; it is driven over the rose beds and shears the bushes to a uniform height. You can do the same thing at home with a pair of hedge clippers or even a chainsaw. The result won't look as neat and tidy, but in a few weeks there'll be so much new growth that you won't notice the difference.

You can use this rough pruning technique on all roses, though do remember that not all of them need a lot of pruning. While it is true that the most commonly grown roses today (the large-flowered bush roses) do best with annual, hard pruning, many of the species roses discussed in this book need little more than tidying up every few years.

The following is a guide to pruning the various types of roses we've covered in this book.

Species Roses and Their Relatives

The prunophobe's dream

Many of these grow into big, billowing shrubs that are covered with flowers and that is their charm. If they are pruned hard annually, as are most modern hybrid roses, you will not get such a terrific display. The species and some other old-fashioned types only need dead or weak growth removed and perhaps some shortening of overlong, wayward shoots. Do the former in late winter when the plants are dormant, and the latter in late spring after the plants have flowered.

If the plant must be reduced in size all over, do this straight after blooming with the hedge clippers, or cut out one-third of all stems at base level. Remove older rather than younger stems. But remember, if you have to do this often you have chosen a species that is too big for your site and you

would be better off replacing it with a rose of a more suitable ultimate size. If you don't need to control the plant's size and it is performing satisfactorily, don't prune it at all.

Climbing Roses

Prune and train them to shape

Climbing roses produce many long canes from their bases. After a few years, growth may become congested and the oldest canes will not be producing as many flowers. Restore vigour by removing a few of the oldest canes completely in winter to make room for new growth. Climbing roses flower on lateral stems off the main cane. If, in spring and summer, these main canes are tied down horizontally, flower-bearing laterals will be produced all along their length. Cutting the roses on long stems (or deadheading on long stems) will encourage the laterals to reshoot.

Weeping Standards

Encouraging weeping

In late winter or early spring cut out a few of the oldest stems entirely. This makes room for vigorous new growth. In summer, trim wayward shoots.

Weeping standards are usually grown with the support of a metal stand which has a central stem and an umbrella-shaped framework at the top. As new canes grow, tie them to the framework to prevent them from thrashing about in the wind and to ensure that they do actually weep.

Groundcover Roses

Bred for rough pruning

The new, long-blooming groundcover roses were bred for landscaping use. They're meant to be massed together to create a carpet of colour, and they're meant to be pruned with a chainsaw or brush-cutter. Simply shear them all over once a year in late winter or early spring.

> ❦
>
> *"You won't kill a rose by pruning it, no matter when or how you do it. "*
>
> ❦

Pruning Roses for Garden Display

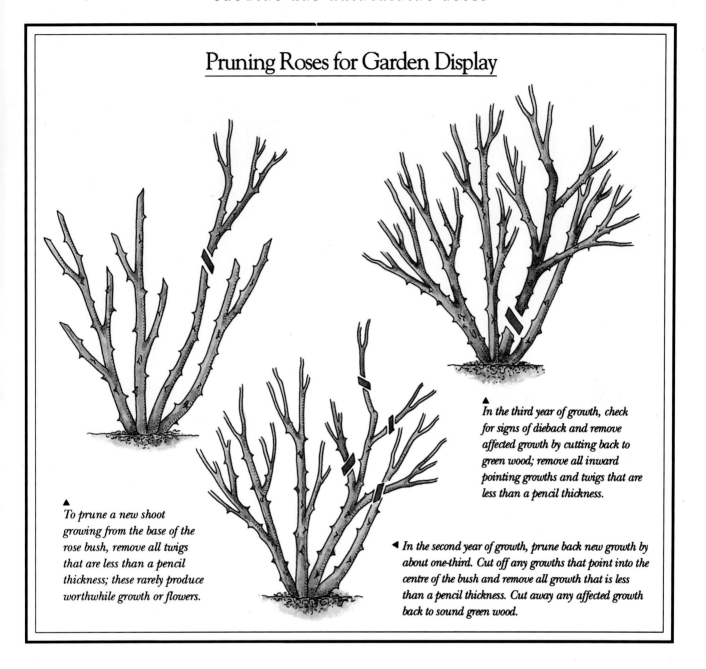

▲
To prune a new shoot growing from the base of the rose bush, remove all twigs that are less than a pencil thickness; these rarely produce worthwhile growth or flowers.

▲
In the third year of growth, check for signs of dieback and remove affected growth by cutting back to green wood; remove all inward pointing growths and twigs that are less than a pencil thickness.

◄ *In the second year of growth, prune back new growth by about one-third. Cut off any growths that point into the centre of the bush and remove all growth that is less than a pencil thickness. Cut away any affected growth back to sound green wood.*

Large-Flowered Bush Roses

Hack them back hard for beautiful blooms

Large-flowered bush roses are by far the most widely planted of all roses. They flower repeatedly from spring to autumn and are best pruned hard in late winter or early spring before the new growth appears, and again but much more lightly, in summer after the first flush of flowers.

You can use hedge clippers (or a chainsaw) and simply slice off the top two-thirds of growth. Or you can opt to do the job in this more traditional but laborious way. Take a pair of very sharp, clean secateurs and, as an anti-bacterial measure, dip the blades in bleach before moving from one plant to the next. For each rose bush, start by cutting out all dead, diseased or spindly growth. Don't leave stubs; cut cleanly to a main branch. Now remove all inward growing stems, then cut back the main branches to a length of about 60cm (2ft) or less. If the bush is a few years old, cut out a few of the oldest stems entirely, right down at the base of the plant. This makes room for vigorous new stems which will in turn produce more flowers. The finished bush should have three to seven stems, depending on its age and size, each growing upwards and outwards.

Clusters of faded apricot-gold blooms decorate the canes of 'William Allen Richardson'. The canes build to compact climbing growth and the plant responds well to light pruning. Dark red with a strong, sweet perfume, 'Chrysler Imperial' (inset), with its compact growth, is a good choice for a standard.

Make all cuts cleanly and at an angle so that the water does not lie on the cut ends. Cut a fraction above an outward pointing bud (a small lump where a leaf joined the stem). Don't prune to an inward pointing bud, or the resulting stem will grow inwards, congesting the centre of the plant.

If there are any stems coming from below the graft union (the slight swelling or bend just above soil level, pull them out rather than cut them. They are from the rootstock onto which the rose was grafted and must not be allowed to take over (or grow at all).

During summer, picking roses on long stems helps to keep the plants compact and in bloom. If you don't wish to pick the flowers, cut them off with long stems when they have faded. At the end of summer, trim off about 30cm (1ft) of growth from all main stems, feed and water deeply and you'll get a beautiful flush of autumn blooms.

A pruning cut with a slope leading away from the bud and one with no ragged edges is the traditional "best practice".

Where no leaves remain to guide you, look closely for dormant buds; these may not be fully developed but pruning will stimulate them to burst into growth.

PRUNING IN PRECIS

- **Prune all dead wood; cut back to sound, healthy, living wood.**
- **Prune all twiggy growth that is not producing flowers.**
- **Each year, prune a few of the oldest trunks right down to the base to encourage and give room for new basal shoots.**
- **Prune any diseased, yellowed or blackened twigs or branches. Cut back to healthy green growth.**
- **Prune any growth that is overhanging pathways or which may otherwise snag adults, children and pets.**

Critter Control

Big animals

Big critters, such as deer, horses, cows, kangaroos, goats, sheep and suchlike, must be kept away if roses are to be grown with happy results. All of the above, plus rabbits and possums, find rose leaves and flowers highly palatable, and none will pass up the chance of browsing among your best rose bushes. If you share your neighbourhood with any of these animals, a fence is a must.

Rabbits and possums

Lowlife, such as rabbits, is more easily controlled by using wire-netting cages for each plant until it is well enough established to take its chances and fight back. Even up the odds for survival with cats or a dog!

If possums are a problem, humane trapping and relocation is the only workable answer. Sprays made of Quassia chips may work for a day or two, if there's no rain, and it may be worthwhile pruning back the treetop pathways that possums use to travel between snacks. But as a rule, if there are possums around, they'll find your roses. Small consolation, perhaps, but possums and rabbits both seem less attracted to very thorny roses.

Parrots and other birds

Parrots and other birds will seek out the new shoots of roses as a source of water in times of drought. The signs are easily recognised: great flocks of screeching multi-coloured birds and dozens of broken rose stems. The birds snap off the watery shoots, chew a short piece to get a few drops of moisture and then discard the shoot in favour of a new one nearby. Flashy strips of aluminium foil or mirror-finish coloured foil streamers across the flight paths of the birds seems to confuse them as they come in to feed, and they go elsewhere to graze. After a few years they learn new landing patterns so outsmart them by laying the strips again in a different pattern.

Pests and Diseases
Some simple preventative measures

Spraying toxic chemicals to control pests and diseases should be a last resort. Prevention being better than a poisonous cure, how can problems with insect pests and diseases of roses be minimised?

The first step is to make sure that the varieties chosen for planting are highly pest and disease resistant. This has been a focus of this book: the roses described are good robust choices.

The second step is not to plant too many roses together; a good mix of flowering shrubs, small trees, climbers, perennials, bulbs and annuals – and

The close jointed growth of Climbing 'Pinkie' makes it a compact climber with dense foliage, prolific blooms, and few prickles!

Don Brice

some roses – will ensure that insect pests and rose diseases do not have so many host plants that they proliferate into a garden problem.

Thirdly, roses are tough plants that have evolved to cope with many of the pests and diseases which afflict them. Certainly don't allow problems to get out of hand, but equally don't reach for the poisons at the first blemish. Given a chance, birds and predatory insects will gobble up many of the problem pests.

Rose Diseases You Should Know

Common rose diseases, such as mildew, black spot and rust, are fungal infections and, while they can all be controlled chemically, you can also do much to prevent their appearance simply by the positioning, spacing and care of your roses.

Full sun and an airy, breezy position, especially in warm, humid climates, helps to minimise the establishment and spread of fungal diseases such as mildew and black spot. That is why it is important not to crowd roses together, or to squeeze them into dense, sheltered shrubberies.

The fungal disease, rust, can be discouraged by the use of a thick, coarse mulch around the rose bushes – straw is ideal. This prevents the rust spores in the soil from being splashed onto the leaves by rain or watering. You can also help new outbreaks from spreading by picking off infected leaves and dropping them in the bin. Don't compost them and don't let them accumulate on the ground under roses.

If fungal diseases start to build up, treat them promptly with a fungicide suitable for the particular problem. If in doubt, take some leaves to a garden nursery and get expert advice on the problem.

The roses listed in this book are largely resistant to mildew, but should it appear, a dusting with fine "flowers of sulphur" when the day is warmest should help control it. Black spot attacks the leaves of all roses, but some are more susceptible to it than others. It is a common problem in areas where the weather is warm and damp, particularly if the foliage stays wet for long after a shower or a hosing. If you find some of your roses are always more infected than others, replace them with more resistant varieties; take your lead from the roses in this book.

Three Pests You're Bound to Meet

Aphids (greenfly) are the most frequently encountered pests on roses. They are most active in spring and so are their natural enemies – the lacewings, hover flies, ladybirds and small birds. You can be a natural enemy too, simply by squashing the insects as they cluster around flowerbuds and new growth or by squirting them away with a jet from the hose. You can also buy additional ladybirds if they are insufficient in your garden when the aphids are present.

If, in the end, the numbers of aphids swell beyond human endurance, use low toxicity sprays such as pyrethrum or home-made garlic-based or soap sprays.

Two-spotted mites (Red spider mites) are a problem in hot, dry weather and, in large numbers, can quickly defoliate roses. In a garden where the roses are not cheek by jowl and have plenty of air circulating around the bushes, a dusting of sulphur will serve to discourage them, as does frequent misting of the undersides of the leaves. You can also buy predatory mites, which devour the pests.

Use chemical miticides as a last resort. These are big-league poisons which require the wearing of protective clothing and mites soon build up resistance to them.

When this occurs, another type of chemical has to be applied. Miticides also kill useful, predatory mites.

Caterpillars, grubs and beetles all like munching on roses, especially on succulent new shoots and tender flower buds. Very often they can be picked off by hand and thrown to the birds or squashed; you can also make simple traps for caterpillars. Tubes of rolled-up cardboard placed in the mulch at the bases of rose bushes become ideal homes for caterpillars. Your job is to evict and squash any residents each morning or so.

Should a plague of caterpillars strike that neither the birds nor you can control, spray with *Bacillus thuringiensis*, a bacteria that affects only caterpillars. Major outbreaks of beetles and bugs will require another chemical, and it is important that you accurately identify the culprits before spraying – garden chemicals are not always effective against all pests, and neither are they suitable for all plants.

SOAP SPRAY

1 tablespoon pure soap flakes or grated Sunlight soap

1 cup boiling water

1 tablespoon white oil

Combine soap flakes and boiling water. Stir until well dissolved. Stir in white oil. Before spraying, dilute mixture with 2 litres of water. Spray as required. Best used when it is made. Clearly label bottle.

Don Brice

118

Tough, disease resistant and vigorous, the groundcover rose 'Raubritter' displays its pink, shell-shaped, cupped flowers in early summer.

PLANT VARIETY RIGHTS

Remember, many new rose varieties are protected by plant patents or plant variety rights. It is illegal to propagate these plants for sale without a license from the owner of the plant variety. Strictly speaking, it is illegal to grow cuttings of these roses for private use in your garden.

PROPAGATING YOUR OWN ROSES

There's one simple way

Propagating roses for your own use or to give to friends is easy and fun, and it's a simple task that anyone can master. Striking roses from cuttings is a quick and easy method. It takes little time or room, and can supply enough rose plants to establish new garden areas. The bushes that are produced by home-grown cuttings will be identical to those from which they were struck, though at first they'll be smaller than commercially propagated plants. After a few years' growth, however, it will be difficult to tell the difference – except that the cutting-grown plants never produce rampant, weedy suckers. Just follow these simple steps:

■ **Cuttings can be taken at any time of year; the most successful times are when the weather is mild rather than very hot or very cold.**

■ **Select cuttings that are about a pencil thickness and of ripened green wood i.e., new growth that has hardened off.**

■ **Take cuttings about 15cm (6in) long; always use a sharp pair of secateurs.**

■ **Six cuttings of one variety should produce at least two rooted plantlets.**

■ **Open a slit trench in a lightly shaded part of the garden, checking to make sure the soil is free of tree and shrub roots. (A slit trench is made by pushing a spade into the soil for its full depth and gently rocking the blade back and forth to make a narrow trench.)**

■ **Trickle some sharp sand (i.e., washed free of small particles and dirt) into the bottom of the trench about 5cm (2in) deep.**

■ **Trim all leaves from the cuttings except for the topmost two sets.**

■ **Dip the cut ends into a softwood rooting hormone powder if you want to improve your chances of success.**

■ **Place the cuttings with the top part upright and with the base planted deep enough for the lowest set of leaves to sit just above the soil level.**

■ **Gently firm the soil back to close the trench.**

■ **Name and date the cuttings with a waterproof, fadeproof tag.**

■ **Water carefully every two or three days, watch for and destroy pests such as slugs and snails.**

■ **Leave alone for at least two months, probably three; remove any cuttings that die; watch for signs of new growth, but do not fertilise to force it. Pull weeds carefully so as not to damage the roots of the cuttings.**

■ **When the plants are making strong new growth, fertilise lightly.**

■ **When the new growth has hardened off, the plants can be transplanted safely. You must water newly-set young plants very diligently until they are fully established.**

■ **Cuttings can be grown in pots following a similar routine. It is advisable to "dibble" planting holes in the potting mix with a pencil and then to gently insert the cutting and firm it in place; about six cuttings per 15cm (6in) pot is right, and make sure the leaves do not touch each other. It should not be necessary to cover the pot with a plastic bag unless you live in a cool, temperate area.**

■ **Cuttings can stay in the ground or pot until it is convenient to plant them out in their permanent positions.**

Don Brice (inset) / Leigh Clapp (left)

Tall and elegant with healthy growth, 'Lady Hillingdon' (left) flowers year round in warm areas. 'Fortune's Double Yellow' (above), another elegant rose, flowers only once a year.

GLOSSARY

Some of the terms used throughout this book are explained here.

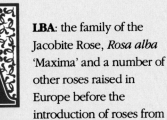**LBA**: the family of the Jacobite Rose, *Rosa alba* 'Maxima' and a number of other roses raised in Europe before the introduction of roses from China. The bushes are characterised by large leaves that are slightly hairy and grey-green in colour. Stems are often densely thorny and rather lax, sprawling outward under the weight of leaves and flowers. The flowers are white, creamy white or soft pink. All varieties flower only once in early summer. Among the best are 'Konegin von Danemark', Felicite Parmentier' and 'Madame Legras de St. Germain'.

APHIDS: very small, winged insects, green, reddish brown or black in colour that appear in large numbers in spring and continue to proliferate throughout summer and autumn. They feed by sucking the sap of plants and are easily controlled by hosing them off with a strong jet of water, by dousing them with soap suds and water or by letting nature take its course – ladybird larvae gobble them up.

BOURBON: a family of large-flowered bush roses that originated on the island of Reunion (I'lle de Bourbon) about 1817. The Bourbons were a family of Spanish and French royalty. Growth tends to be tall and lax, making them ideal as small climbers. The flowers are typically large, well-scented and packed with many petals arranged in cupped and quartered style.

BUDDED ROSES: most roses sold commercially are two separate kinds of rose grafted together; a topmost branch structure of a variety that will produce beautiful flowers and a root system and trunk (or stem) that is strong-growing and very hardy; together the roots and the truck are called the "understock" or "root stock". To produce such a plant, a single, dormant growing bud of a fine-flowered variety is grafted (inserted) into a small cut just under the bark of the understock and firmly bound with soft tape. This process is called "budding". After several months the bud and understock unite, then the bud grows rapidly, eventually flowering and developing into a bushy plant.

CHINA ROSES: roses that have their origins in the garden forms of *Rosa chinensis*. The first of these were collected in the gardens of southern China and hybridised by European rose breeders in the 18th and 19th centuries. *Rosa chinensis* has never been found growing in the wild. The glowing scarlets, coral pinks, muted yellows and apricot shades of the flowers delighted collectors and breeders with a range of colours not found in the old European roses. The repeat-flowering habit of the china roses introduced the genetic potential for breeding the ever-blooming roses we value today. Growth is densely twiggy and virtually evergreen; plants are susceptible to cold and frost, but in warmer climates will grow and flower year-round. Plants left unpruned, and undamaged by frost, will slowly build up to over 2m (6.5ft) tall and as much across.

FLORIBUNDA ROSES: a group of 20th century cluster-flowered roses that were originally fairly low, spreading growers noted for their prolific bloom and sparkling, clear colours. Hybridised with Hybrid Tea roses, their offspring developed ever larger flowers until the distinctions between the two groups became lost in a further group that were labelled, "Grandifloras". Mainly intended for mass plantings in parks and public gardens, the best varieties have sturdy habits, disease and pest resistant foliage and a multitude of flowers produced over five to six months.

FLOWERS OF SULPHUR: or "dusting sulphur" is a fine form of crystalline sulphur that is used to help control fungal attacks on rose leaves, especially mildew. It is best applied in the evening on a warm day by shaking it into the centre and underside of the bushes from a flour shaker or coarse muslin bag. It also has a mild, acidifying effect on soils and is said to promote micro-organisms that help decompose compost and mulches.

FORMS: seedlings of wild (species) roses of uncertain breeding,

*1. Quartered rosette,
e.g., 'Mme Isaac Pereire'.*

*2. Flat,
e.g., **Rosa chinensis** 'Mutabilis'.*

*3. Urn-shaped,
e.g., 'Fragrant Cloud'.*

*4. Pompom,
e.g., 'Tricolore de Flandre'.*

*5. Cupped,
e.g., 'Le Vésuve'.*

*6. Rounded,
e.g., 'Paul Neyron'.*

FLOWER SHAPES

*7. Pointed,
e.g., 'Dr Grill'.*

*8. Rosette,
e.g., 'Sexy Rexy'.*

self-pollinated or hybridised with other roses by bees. *Rosa Moyesii* 'Geranium' is an example. Found as a seedling in the garden of Sir Frederick Stern and introduced by him, it is not known what its parents were, although one was obviously *Rosa Moyesii*.

FOUND ROSES: roses that have been found by collectors of antique rose varieties growing in derelict cemeteries and abandoned gardens. As it is impossible to accurately identify the thousands of old roses introduced during the 18th and 19th centuries from the few paintings and brief descriptions that survive, the roses are usually called "foundlings" or "found" roses, and given a name that identifies where it was

found, e.g., 'Burgdorf's Farm' rose or 'Gnadenfrei Cemetery' rose.

GALLICA ROSES: old European roses that were bred before the introduction of Chinese rose varieties. They make low thicketing shrubs with upright, thin branches, many small bristles and spines, but few thorns. Foliage is usually dark green, leathery and dull, rather than shiny with small, even serrations around the edge of each leaf. They sucker very freely when grown on their own roots. Gallicas flower only once each year in early summer.

GRAFTED: see "budded roses".

GRANDIFLORA: a group of 20th century roses with very large flowers and strong habits of growth; they are

derived from the Hybird Teas and are considered by many authorities to be genetically identical to them. A good example is 'Queen Elizabeth'.

HARDENED OFF: is a term that relates to the stage of maturation that follows the emergence of new growth. New growth is very soft and filled with sap; it is said to be "soft growth". As the growth ripens in the sun, the new leaves and stems become hard to the touch, though they remain pliable and green. At this stage growth is described as "hardened off". The same term is applied to plants grown from cuttings. When the developing plants no longer wilt when the day becomes hot, they are said to have "hardened off".

HARDY: drought-tolerant.

HEALTHY: disease resistant and having vigour enough to be easily grown and to produce a good display of flowers without lots of feeding, spraying and fussing.

HEAVING: happens when new rose bushes are planted in autumn in cold climates and do not make strong, active root growth before the ground freezes. In this circumstance, the new rose will be lifted out of the soil by the repeated action of the frost freezing the ground and thawing. Heaving can result in the dehydration of the plant, cracking and splitting of the bark, frost burn or, most likely, death through freezing of the plant and its roots. It can be avoided by planting container grown roses in spring or summer.

HIPS: the fruits of the rose bush.

HYBRID PERPETUAL: a group of 19th century roses with a fairly reliable repeat-blooming habit, i.e., crops of flowers are produced two or three times during each growing season. Generally speaking, the flowers are larger than those of old, European roses and the repeat-blooming habit was a breeding breakthrough that led to the Hybrid Tea down to the continuously flowering modern shrub roses.

HYBRID TEA: a group of 20th century roses noted for their large flowers, long season of bloom and wide range of colours. The flower form is a pointed bud that opens to show a regular arrangement of petals evenly distributed around a high centre of closed petals. This form of flower is regarded as the acme of perfection by competition exhibitors in rose shows. The bushes tend to be stiffly upright with a canopy of foliage with a show of bare, thorny branches beneath. Growth can be tall, about 2m (6.5ft) and more, but plants are generally kept lower by hard pruning when the bushes are dormant.

MOUNDING: refers to the practice in cold climates, where there is the risk of winter damage to roses by freezing of the canes or frost burn, of "mounding" the dormant rose plants with a thick layer of insulating material, such as dry leaves, straw or bracken (see "winterising").

NOISETTE ROSES: a group of shrubs and compact climbers that originated in Charleston, South Carolina in about 1802. A seedling was raised from a Chinese rose ('Parsons' Pink') which had been bought from a French nurseryman, Phillipe Noisette, of Charleston. Noisette raised more seedlings from the first seedling and one of these was sent to his brother, Louis, who had a nursery in Paris. From these a race of fine garden roses has been developed.

OLD EUROPEAN ROSES: old garden roses bred before the introduction of the repeat-blooming china roses. Typically the old European roses bloom only once a year in early summer.

OLD-FASHIONED ROSE: this term usually describes a flower form in which the petals are folded and quartered, as in a Danish pastry, or cupped and quartered in which the outer petals form a "cup" arrangement around the quartered central petals. In general, they are roses of the 19th century or before.

OWN-ROOT ROSES: roses that are grown from cuttings instead of being budded onto an understock. The flowering bush and it's root system are all part of the same plant; therefore any suckers that are produced will have flowers that are identical to the "mother" plant from which it has grown. Own-root roses are preferred by some gardeners.

PEGGED: see "tied down".

POLYANTHA ROSES: a group of low, cluster-flowered roses which are prolific and colourful. They were popular in the late 19th century and the early years of the 20th century. Many varieties produce extremely large heads of bloom with many buds that enable a long period of flowering.

QUASSIA CHIPS: the dried and shredded bark of an African tree available from pharmacists. When soaked in water, according to directions given on the packet, chemicals are released which have a very repellent, bitter flavour that deters possums and rabbits from nibbling on plants sprayed with it. It is short lived once sprayed, being washed off by rain or sprinklers.

ROOT STOCK: see "budded roses".

SINGLE, SEMI-DOUBLE AND DOUBLE FLOWERS: there are those pedants who actually count the number of petals a rose may have, but even this pseudo-scientific approach doesn't help to clarify any perceived differences. Strictly speaking, a rose with two rows of petals is a "double" rose, since botanically, roses have only one row. However, gardeners would regard this as "semi-single" or "semi-double" or "slightly double". A rose with three or four rows of petals could be "double" if the petals stood high and were ruffled so that the centre of the flower was obscured, or it could be "semi-double" if the petals were laid flat and the centre of the flower was exposed.

SPECIES ROSES: roses that occur naturally in the wild. These roses vary from massive climbers from

subtropical Myanmar (Burma), to dwarf, scrubby bushes from the semi-desert regions of the northern hemisphere; yet others range from the coast of England to the shores of Alaska. Most roses are deciduous shrubs, although a few are virtually evergreen, and nearly all are armed with thorns, bristles and spines. Their varied form, easy culture and delightful flowers offer a rich field of possibilities for breeders.

SPORT: a rose which has grown as a distinct vegetative mutation of a known rose variety. The form of growth may vary considerably from the parent plant, e.g., a bush rose may throw a climbing sport, or a massive climber, such as 'Mermaid', may produce a miniature version of itself, e.g., 'Happenstance'. Sometimes it is only the flower that is varied by a change in colour, or more rarely by the development of striped blooms. And sometimes the foliage may become variegated with blotches or stripes of white or pale yellow.

STANDARD: a rose which has been budded onto a tall, single stem of understock so as to produce a flowering bush on top of a single trunk. Such plants are very useful for creating formal gardens, especially when planted in pairs or double rows by doorways, gates or along paths. Standards are usually available in three heights: approximately 50cm for miniature roses, 85cm for large-flowered bush roses and 1.8m for standards of climbing roses that are trained as weeping roses. Sometimes standards are called stem roses.

SUCKERS: new, growing shoots that appear from below ground level near the base of an established rose plant. In nature this habit of growth is one means by which many roses multiply and spread; in gardens suckers that

appear are usually unwanted growths from the root system of the understock. These should be carefully dug around to expose where they are shooting from and then pulled out with a sharp, hard tug. Own-root roses produce suckers that are new plants identical to the nearby parent plant.

TEA ROSES: a group of large-flowered roses hybridised in Europe during the 19th century from a quartet of large-flowered Chinese garden roses. They grow into large, shrubby bushes and flower over a long period from late spring until late

> ❧
> *"Strictly speaking, a rose with two rows of petals is a 'double' rose, since, botanically, roses have only one row."*
> ❧

autumn. Generally, they have a fine, delicate perfume. There are also some climbing forms.

TIED DOWN: a means of training roses to grow low to the ground by tying the canes to "pegs" (usually short pieces of slender, forked-tree branches, or old wire coat hangers cut and unbent, that resemble tent pegs). By pulling rose canes down and tying them into a lateral position, the formation of short, flowering side shoots is increased.

TWO-SPOTTED MITE: minute insects which can hardly be seen by the human eye. Their presence is

indicated by a fine webbing on the undersides of the leaves that is speckled with tiny red bodies. They can be brought under control by spraying a fine mist onto the undersides of the leaves with a hose or by dusting with "Flowers of Sulphur". In extreme cases, they can be treated with a systemic insecticide.

VIGOROUS: means growth is sufficient to maintain branch, foliage and flower production appropriate to the characteristics of the group, e.g., climbers produce enough growth to climb. If this doesn't happen due to the plant being weak or planted in a bad situation, it fails to thrive and "goes back".

WILD ROSES: see "species roses".

WINTERISING: refers to the the burying of dormant rose plants in a thick layer of insulating material, such as dry leaves, straw or bracken, to safeguard against winter damage to roses by freezing of the canes or frost burn. The material is kept in place by a burlap-covered frame of wood or wire mesh. At the first sign of heavy frost, the plants are lightly tip pruned and covered with a mound of insulating material; if necessary, the long canes of some shrubs and climbers are tied together and then buried. As spring approaches and the threat of severe frosts abates, the insulating material can be removed, but it must be kept nearby (in case frosty nights return when it should be piled on again). With the arrival of milder weather, the plants can be left unprotected; they will begin to show signs of growth and, at this time, dead wood and unwanted canes can be pruned off safely.

INDEX